WineTrails
OF IDAHO

A guide for uncorking your memorable wine tour

by
Steve
Roberts

SOUTH SLOPE
PRODUCTIONS

IDAHO

WineTrails NW

WineTrails of Idaho
A guide for uncorking your memorable wine tour

Published by
South Slope Productions
9311 SE 36th Street, Suite 108, Mercer Island, WA 98040

Library of Congress Cataloging-in-Publication Data available.

 WineTrails Northwest logo by Beth Hayes, King Salmon Creative Designs
Updated by Lisa J. Pettit, Lisa Pettit Designs

Edited by Sunny Parsons

Cover and interior design by Lisa J. Pettit, Lisa Pettit Designs

Photos by Steve Roberts, South Slope Productions, unless indicated otherwise

3-Horse Ranch - Photo of Gary Cunningham by Warren Lassen
Wedding Tent - Photo courtesy of Woodriver Cellars

Editorial assistant, Meg Roberts

Layout and production by Seattle Publishing, Inc.

First Edition

ISBN 13 - 978-0-9792698-2-0

Printed in the United States by Consolidated Press.

Acknowledgements & Dedication

My travels throughout the Gem State introduced me to a bumper crop of winemaking talent, including former orchardists, degreed enology students, restaurateurs, doctors, lawyers and other professionals, all with résumés that include extensive winemaking experience in California, Washington and/or other countries. The diversity of their experiences and backgrounds has brought to fruition a wide range of red and white wines that appeal to a host of palates. To me, however, their collective passion has brought about some mighty fine wine and I am thrilled to be the recipient of such delicious nectar. To them I say a heartfelt "Thank you."

Center stage in nurturing this industry is the Idaho Grape Growers & Wine Producers Commission, with Moya Shatz at its helm. Her youthful energy is emblematic of the state's wine industry, and I am indebted to her for sharing the wine-industry landscape in the early phases of my research.

I would be remiss if I didn't mention the talented team of professionals assembled by South Slope Productions to produce this book. It begins with the design of the book. To that end, I am forever grateful to artist extraordinaire Lisa J. Pettit. Lisa designed the eye-catching cover as well as the stunning interior layout. However, of equal importance is the "heavy-lifting" work associated with editing the manuscript. To that end, I am eternally grateful to copy editor Sunny Parsons. The actual production of the book is the work of a very gifted team of professionals at Seattle Publishing. They had the daunting task of flowing text, photos, maps and Lisa's icons into the book's layout. This work requires many days, singular attention to detail and quad lattes. In the background of all this is my production partner and spouse, Kathleen Roberts. Throughout the journey, she was my constant companion and collaborative partner.

Finally, I wish to dedicate WineTrails of Idaho to the future of the Idaho wine industry. Although the industry is being led by a very capable army of winemaking professionals, it is easy to imagine some energetic food-science student attending classes at the University of Idaho or a kid in Pocatello studying soil samples, both destined to become tomorrow's Idaho winemakers. This next generation will take Idaho to still greater heights in the production of consistent, premium-quality wines. To them I say, "Happy WineTrails!"

Sandpoint
Coeur d'Alene
Kellogg
90
Moscow
Lewiston
12
12
Idaho
95
Payette
Idaho City
75
Boise
Nampa
Ketchum
Hailey
20
Rexburg
Idaho Falls
Blackfoot
Pocatello
84
Twin Falls
Burley
85
84
15

Table of Contents

Bitner Vineyards

Frenchman's Gulch Winery

Snake-smitten — Idaho's Surprising Wines

"Idaho?" was the common refrain I heard when I told people I was working on a guidebook for the Gem State. There followed the proverbial "Boy, that's going to be a pretty skinny book," accompanied by raised eyebrows and a chuckle or two. Lest they suggest that I voluntarily commit myself to the nearest mental health facility, I would respond by saying, "Well, did you know that Idaho has about 40 wineries?" That seemed to give them pause for thought and allowed me time to add that Idaho has a newly designated American Viticultural Area: the Snake River Valley. At this point, most began to warm to the idea that Idaho might be worth checking out. But truth be told, fellow WineTrail trekkers, even I had my doubts. Sure, I had tasted wines from Ste. Chapelle Winery, Sawtooth Winery and Frenchman's Gulch Winery in Ketchum, where I live for part of the year, but I was clueless about the rest of Idaho's growing number of wineries.

Along the Boise River

That was before I became enlightened — before I tossed camera and notebook in my car and hit the back roads of Idaho's wine country, before I caught sight of the bud-breaking vineyards in the Snake River Valley and met the winemakers. Be assured we're not talking sweet fruit wines here. Not to say you can't find Idaho wines with high residual sugar levels, but these are Bordeaux- and Rhône-style wines that compete toe to toe with other quality America wines. And one huge advantage to wine-trekking through Idaho is that you don't have to battle the hordes of other wine tourists you would encounter in Napa or on a Thanksgiving weekend in the Willamette Valley. Along Idaho's uncrowded byways, you might be the only visitor to a winery during your tasting stop. The experience is intimate, friendly and genuine. Stopping to sample an Idaho winery's wares, you're likely to meet the winemaker, scratch the belly of the family dog and leave touting an unexpected case of wine to the car. Well, at least that was my experience, and I am willing to bet a bottle of Snake River Valley's finest that will be yours, too.

Let's face it, when you think of Pacific Northwest wine-producing states, the Gem State comes in a distant third behind Washington and Oregon. As John Thorngate, a former professor at the University of Idaho who is now on the faculty at the University of California, Davis, stated, "In Idaho, we're the oft forgotten 'other' state in the Pacific Northwest." Ironically, the state has a rich history in winemaking and had racked up a number of awards before Prohibition put the big kibosh on the wine trade.

Life's pleasures

Robert Wing, in his well-researched 1990 "History of Wine in Lewiston" article that he wrote for the Nez Perce County Historical Society, tells of French-born Louis Delsol bringing the first grapes into the Clearwater Valley in 1872. There followed another Frenchman to the area, Robert Schleicher, who planted an estimated 80 acres of premium wine grapes sometime in the early 1900s. Concurrently, a German-born transplant by the name of Jacob Schaefer also planted vines and made wine in the Lewiston-Clarkston area. These three men shaped the early Idaho wine industry and won awards in far-flung places like Omaha, Buffalo and St. Louis. It's ironic that it wasn't a drought, a cold snap or the dreaded phylloxera (or "grape louse") that spelled the demise of this fledgling Idaho wine industry, but the national temperance movement, whose campaign led to the institution of Prohibition in 1920, the "Great Experiment" that criminalized the manufacture and consumption of alcohol.

Once Prohibition ended in 1933, Idaho was slow to recover focusing on other agriculture products like wheat, potatoes and fruit trees. However, by the 1990s, a fusion of economic and political events (including Boise economic boom in the 1980s and 1990s, which brought people from other parts of the country with a penchant for fine wine) occurred to jump-start the 'other' state. Changing palates, Boise's renaissance and a growing pool of excellent winemaking talent had all conspired to put Idaho on the watch list of premium wine-producing states. But it was the federal government's designation of the Snake River Valley as an official American Viticultural Area, or AVA, in 2007 that juiced Idaho. Such a label is like a straight shot of adrenaline in terms of creating brand awareness. Goodbye potato, hello cabernet… sort of.

Idaho's Hidden Wine Country Regions

Snake River Valley is positioned center stage for Idaho's wine industry. Located in southwestern Idaho (and spilling into eastern Oregon), this massive AVA comprises 8,263 square miles or 5.27 million acres. That's about the size of New Jersey! However, only about 1,100 acres of grapes are in production in the appellation — a relative drop in the land bucket. So for those desiring to start a new life and plant a vineyard, think Idaho.

The fact is, southern Idaho offers ideal growing conditions for vinifera grape varieties because of its high elevation, low moisture, well-drained volcanic ash soils and northerly latitude (43 degrees north), which fosters a long growing season. Yes, location is crucial, and finding the right microclimate in the Snake River Valley is essential to lessen the effect of severe cold weather. Although

wine grapes thrive in this four-season climate, there are the occasional deep freezes, which turn vines black and ruin a year's crop. But even Idaho's cold winters can be a plus, forcing vines to go dormant to conserve carbohydrates needed for growth and keeping the dreaded phylloxera at bay. Fortunately, many locations within the Snake

Thousand Springs Winery

River Valley provide a moderating influence, cooling the vineyards during the summer months and sloughing off the cold air during the winter. During the summer, the region's combination of cool nights and hot days provides a needed "diurnal" effect to balance the grapes' acids and sugars.

The Snake River Valley's frost-free period, which defines the viticultural growing season, extends from approximately mid-May to the end of September — relatively short in viticultural terms, but still long enough to get the sugar (i.e., brix) and acid balance just right for picking most of the time. The average growing season for the Snake River Valley AVA is 142 days — much shorter than Oregon's Umpqua Valley AVA 218 days, and the Walla Walla Valley AVA, which enjoys 206 days.

It's a given that plants need water, but in the high desert of southern Idaho, water is a major concern. Thus, irrigation is of paramount importance for growing grapes in this region. On the other hand, unlike their counterparts

Sawtooth Winery

in Western Washington or Oregon's Willamette Valley, the grape growers of Idaho don't spend sleepless nights fretting about mold and mildew from moisture-laden air.

Historically, many Idaho winemakers have relied on grapes procured from Washington vineyards. Over many vintages, these winemakers have established close working relationships with Washington's grape growers, enjoying consistent fruit year after year. What's more, many Idaho wineries — particularly those in northern Idaho — are in closer proximity to Washington's Columbia Valley, making it easier logistically to obtain grapes from that AVA. But that arrangement is beginning to change. Look for more Idaho wine labels bearing the Snake River Valley appellation as more acreage comes under production and the grape growers evolve in terms of their viticultural practices. I know that when I spot a bottle of Idaho wine at my favorite wine shop, I look for the Snake River Valley appellation designation on the front label. Idaho wines made from Idaho grapes may not be de rigueur yet, but they will be. Now's the time to try these vanguard wines

Although the Snake River Valley AVA is currently the only federally designated viticultural area in Idaho, expect that to change with the emergence of the Clearwater Valley viticultural area in the Lewiston-Clarkston Valley. A group of wine growers in the Lewiston-Clarkston area is spearheading an effort to win federal approval for this viticulture area. As noted above, French and German immigrants successfully planted European vines in the 1800s in the Clearwater Valley area, and today we are seeing a number of vineyards being cultivated in the valley. Indeed, these are heady times for north-central Idaho, and this geographically stunning area just may be the prime spot for any wannabe dirt guys with a burning desire to grow grapes.

How to Use This Guidebook

To make Idaho easier to digest, I divvied up the state into three distinct "Wine Country Regions":

1. Panhandle Wine Country — essentially from north-central Idaho (Lewiston) to the Canadian border

2. Snake River Valley Wine Country West — the area surrounding Boise and the rich farmland of Nampa and Caldwell west to the Oregon border

3. Snake River Valley Wine Country East — the large area east of Boise to Twin Falls and north to Ketchum/Sun Valley

Within each of these wine country regions, I have organized "public" wineries into a group that can be visited in a day or two following a commonsense route. I call these routes WineTrails. By "public wineries" I mean those wineries that have a tasting room that is open to the public for part or all of the year. We're not necessarily talking open to the public seven days a week — some wineries are open on weekends only and for just a portion of the year, others are open year-round, and still others may have regular hours posted, but a family emergency or the opening of hunting season could change things. So pay particular attention to winery hours noted in *Wine Trails of Idaho* and call ahead to be sure they'll be welcoming visitors.

Ste. Chapelle Winery

Other wineries featured in this book are open by appointment only and not part of a particular WineTrail. The appointment-only wineries are wonderful to visit — just call well in advance.

Each wine country region has at least one WineTrail to tour. For the Panhandle Wine Country, I have chosen the name North Idaho WineTrail for the four wineries included in this tour. No, it's not a sexy name, but you don't have to guess where it is. The Snake River Valley Wine Country West boasts two distinct WineTrails: the Sunnyslope WineTrail in southwest Idaho, and the Boise Area WineTrail. Between the two, there are a dozen wineries to visit and clearly represent the heart and soul of Idaho's $70 million wine industry. The fourth and final WineTrail is Snake River Valley Wine Country East, which includes five truly remarkable wineries. Because these wineries are, for the most part, situated in the Thousand Springs Scenic Byway, it is only fitting that I chose the name Thousand Springs WineTrail.

Please be aware that this guidebook is a snapshot in time. Things change. New wineries open, tasting-room hours change, winemakers move on, and a new puppy could even replace the old winery dog. For this reason, I offer a caveat that applies throughout the book: Call ahead! By doing so, you ensure that the

winery will be open and that its wines are still in stock. From personal experience, I know what it is like to drive more than 100 miles to visit a particular winery, only to discover that it has sold out of its wines. Bummer!

Harvest time at 3 Horse Ranch Vineyards

Don't make that mistake — call ahead. Second, check out WineTrailsnw.com for the most current information regarding the winery you wish to visit. Every attempt is made to keep the site up to date. In addition, WineTrailsnw.com is also a good source for wine-event information. Many wineries have regular events (e.g., Ste. Chapelle's popular concert series, Woodriver Cellar's live music weekends or Pend d'Oreille Winery's frequent musical gigs), and WineTrailsnw. com or individual winery websites are good sources for event information when planning your wine tour getaway.

Ready, Set, Swirl!

It's a cardinal rule of mine to be open, and I advise WineTrail trekkers to do the same. Don't rule out visiting a winery housed in a doublewide trailer. Often, those can be the most fun. If the tasting fee is a nominal amount, spring for it. You have traveled a great distance to get there, and the $5 tasting fee allows your taste buds to experience a full range of wines. Besides that, the tasting fees are usually waived with the purchase of wine.

Be open to different styles of winemaking. There is no one right way to make wine, and over the course of a few thousand years, many winemaking styles have emerged. One such example featured in this book is the sur lie style of winemaking employed by James Holesinsky at Holesinsky Winery in Buhl. Check out his syrah and tell me you don't taste the intense blackberry, black pepper and cassis aromas. This syrah's layered flavors and long finish had me begging for another pour. Another example is Woodriver Cellars port. Aged in whiskey barrels for several years, this slightly sweet wine had me mentally pairing it with pound cake, classical music and a cigar (although I don't smoke!). I wasn't expecting such a treat and was pleasantly surprised. Again, jettison preconceived notions and allow yourself to experience something out of the ordinary. With just one sip, you may become a convert.

Besides the "call ahead" advice I've already given, my travels have reinforced four other key to-dos before venturing out on a wine tour:

(1) Bring cash for tasting fees
(2) Take along a cooler to transport wine in hot weather
(3) Bring water and
(4) Take along a map or GPS device.

In the next section, Practical Stuff — Planning Your Wine Tour Getaway, I offer information for planning your Idaho wine tour, helpful hints for traveling with kids and pets, tips on bicycling in wine country and advice for those who wish to get married at a winery. Phone numbers, along with website and email addresses, are provided. But perhaps the most important advice I can give to anyone is to designate a driver before hitting the WineTrail, or least pace yourself — those ounces add up. And know that it's fine to spit or dump; that's what those receptacles on top of the tasting-room bar are for. Drink responsibly. Drive responsibly.

And by all means, take along this guidebook and read aloud as you sip and swirl your way through wine country! It includes maps and driving directions to aid you, and tasting-room hours and WineTrail tips are sprinkled throughout. Oh, and make a point of asking the winemaker for his or her autograph. Winemakers love it and take great pleasure in signing their page in the book.

Happy WineTrails!

Steve Roberts, the WineTrails Guy

Practical Stuff —
Planning Your Wine Tour Getaway

Statewide Resources

Travel Idaho
www.visitidaho.org

AAA of Oregon/Idaho
Serving members in Oregon and
southern Idaho
800-444-8091
www.aaaorid.com

AAA of Washington/Idaho
Serving members in
Washington and northern
Idaho
www.aaawa.com

Alaska Airlines —
City Guides
800-ALASKAAIR
www.alaskaair.com

Idaho Grape Growers
and Wine Producers Com-
mission
info@idahowines.org
www.idahowines.org

WineTrails NW Website
Companion website to this
guidebook; provides latest winery and
wine-event information
800-533-6165
info@winetrailsnw.com
www.winetrailsnw.com

Getting Around

Airport locations
Ketchum/Sun Valley
Lewiston
Moscow/Pullman
Spokane, Wash.
Twin Falls

Interstate highways
There are two major interstates
that run through Idaho: I-84 in the
southern part of the state
and I-90 in northern
Idaho, along with many
state highways that can
take you from north to
south and all around.

One of Idaho's extraordinary
scenic byways

511 Service
511 service offers
information on road
conditions, road-
construction updates
and weather, as well as
tourism information,
state parks and recreation
information, scenic byways and a
historical-marker guide. As you are
traveling to or through Idaho, you
can dial 511 and be connected with
this service, or check it out online at
www.511.idaho.gov.

North Idaho Bed & Breakfast
Association
www.bba.travel

Wine Touring and Wheelchair Access

An increasing number of wine-tasting rooms in the Pacific Northwest are becoming wheelchair accessible. Being wheelchair friendly means that the winery designates special parking spaces for cars bearing wheelchair placards, there are no stairs to impede access, wide doors have been constructed for easy access and restrooms meet ADA standards.

Many Idaho wineries — particularly the newer ones — are sensitive to this issue and many of them have designed or redesigned their facilities to accommodate disabled travelers.

Even if the winery indicates that it is wheelchair accessible, we believe it is a good idea to call ahead if you have any concerns. For example, if you have a van that is specially equipped for loading and unloading a wheelchair, you may be apprehensive about having enough

Indian Creek Winery

room in the parking lot to accommodate this operation. When attending a special event such as a winemaker dinner or a wedding, there may be wheelchair access to the tasting room, but what about the rest of the winery, bathroom facilities and outside among the vineyards? Call or email the winery should you have any such concerns.

For general information to assist disabled travelers, check out these websites:
- Access-Able Travel Source — www.access-able.com
- Global Access Disabled Travel Network — www.globalaccessnews.com
- Mobility International — www.miusa.org

Wine Touring with Pets

"Pets Welcome" is a sign not often see at wineries. In fact, most wineries don't welcome dogs into the tasting room. Too many things can go wrong. Picture a counter-surfing dog scarfing on crackers and cheese trays or getting into a scrap with the winery cat.

Ironically, a large percentage of wineries do have a winery dog, which has led to an explosion of coffee-table books featuring mug shots of winery pooches.

However, even though a winery might be dog friendly toward its own pooch, introducing your dog into the tasting room is bound to create territorial issues.

However, if you do bring Fido along on your next wine tour, you will find a

Indian Creek Winery's Dahlia

number of hotels and quaint country inns that welcome pets. Some may charge an additional fee, but typically it's a nominal amount.

When traveling with a canine companion pack doggy snacks and water, and allow for pit stops along the way. Always keep the window open and park in the shade, especially in hot weather, to avoid baking your dog. In the summertime, it's dangerous to keep a dog in a car, even with windows open, especially in hot wine country regions such as Sunnyslope and Lewiston. Bottom line: Take your dog to the park, not to the winery.

Wine Touring with Kids

As a general rule, wineries are not set up to handle little tykes — after all, these establishments are "no whining zones." The stacked bottles of wine and Riedel crystal are easy targets for a wandering 3-year-old. Few wineries offer a play area in the tasting room or a playground outside for kids to enjoy. When they do, it is often more of a distraction for parents, who are trying to swirl and sip. However, if you do have your children along and insist on checking out a winery or two, here are a few tips to make it a family-friendly experience.

First, make the trip informational and choose wineries that feature a wine tour. Treat it like a field trip and discover how wine is made. At harvest time, it is not unusual to see kids stomping grapes (talk about cheap labor). The smiles on their faces are testament to their glee.

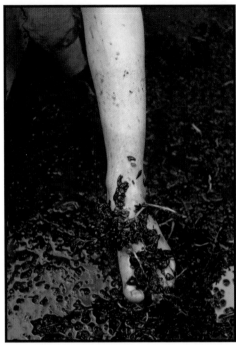
Crush at Frenchman's Gulch Winery

Try to combine wine tasting with family activities such as picnicking at the winery, checking out a hands-on museum or going on a nature hike. Involve the kids in the planning. Sure, you're picking up the tab, but if you attend to their needs, it's easier for them to accommodate you.

Don't attempt more than a couple of wineries in a day. Dragging kids to more than one or two wineries is a surefire way to quash a good day.

Finally, if your intent is to make a day of wine tasting, consider splitting up. Dad takes the kids the first day and enjoys kid-friendly activities, while mom checks out three or four must-see wineries. Perhaps on day two, it's dad's turn to sample his favorite wineries, while mom has the kids. Divide and conquer!

There's plenty to do in wine country for families. However, to make it truly memorable, you need to plan ahead and create a win-win situation for both yourselves and the kids.

Bicycling in Wine Country

Looking to minimize your carbon footprint in wine country? How about forgoing the car in favor of your bike? Sipping and cycling in wine country is more than a pipe dream. In the Pacific Northwest, choices abound for riding alongside lush vineyards and sampling amazing wines. What better way to work off some calories while taking in some much needed refreshment in the form of reds and whites? It's the ol' input-output equation: By the end of the day, you break even calorie-wise, but gain immeasurably in life's pleasures.

Idaho offers many a bike-touring treasure. For additional information, check out the state's transportation website at www.itd.idaho.gov/bike_ped. Download or request a Scenic Byway map that includes Snake River Byway, Thousand Springs Byway and Lake Coeur d'Alene Byway.

An excellent regional resource for planning your bike tours can be found at www.bicyclepaper.com. At this website, "everything biking" abounds with news and event information, including a number of rides that take you through the heart of wine country. If you're looking for an experienced touring company that provides fully supported bike touring (i.e., from boxed lunches to overnight accommodations), check out www.bicycleadventures.com.

A word of caution is in order here: Riding a bicycle is potentially dangerous. It's often not the cyclists' riding behavior that endangers them, but the car driver's inability to see the cyclists or to exercise caution while

Hells Canyon Winery

negotiating around them. Adding alcohol only compounds the danger. Cyclists need to have a tasting strategy — either sip and spit with great frequency or sample one or two wines at each winery and limit the number of tasting rooms you visit. Alternatively, plan your biking for the morning and leave the wine tasting for the afternoon. Drink responsibly; ride responsibly.

Getting Married in Wine Country

"I do."

With those two words, you can finally relax, knowing that the months of planning are over. The flowers you chose, the colors selected for the dresses, and the vows you wrote and rewrote are behind you. Now you can loosen your tie or adjust that strapless bra and let loose — after all, you're in the heart of wine country and there is cabernet sauvignon awaiting your drinking pleasure.

Getting hitched at a winery is gaining popularity throughout the Northwest. Wineries offer a quiet retreat for couples to share a special day with friends and family. What's more, an increasing number are becoming "destination wineries" for weddings, complete with creature comforts such as a spa for working out those wedding-day muscle aches, overnight lodging with smelly soaps, picturesque ponds stocked with koi and, of course, a cellar with library (reserved) wines. Idaho offers a number of wineries that welcome weddings, including Snyder Winery, Indian Creek Winery, Carmela Vineyards, Sawtooth Winery, Ste. Chapelle Winery and Woodriver Cellars. All are great choices for outdoor weddings from May through September.

If you have your hearts set on exchanging vows in wine country, a word to the wise: Once you have established your wedding criteria (i.e., budget and size), nail down the winery setting as soon as possible. Booking a winery a year prior to the big day is key to securing these very popular venues!

To reduce the risk of winery wedding plans going awry, I offer up a three-step process sure to guarantee success.

Sawtooth Winery

1. **Choose the location.** Wineries can accommodate wedding parties of varying sizes, from just two (can you say "elope"?) to perhaps even a couple of hundred well-wishers, depending on the individual winery. In this case, size matters. If you want a wedding that has a guest list approaching 250, most wineries can't accommodate that size — they lack the parking facilities and the lawn space for chairs, or their postage-stamp-size dance floors are too small to contain Uncle Willy's busting a move. If you are looking at a destination winery, consider the number of out-of-town guests attending and whether or not the winery and nearby inns/resorts have the space to accommodate those numbers.

Once you have selected potential sites for your wedding, plan on visiting each one and speaking with its wedding/event coordinator. These folks have a wealth of information and can readily answer your questions concerning costs and availability for your big day. Imagine how the winery may look (or feel like) in the particular month of your ceremony and during the morning or evening. Consider the elements: the chance of rain, the sunlight for photography (best in the morning or early evening) and the wind. If high winds are likely, you may want to rethink the idea of a "unity" candle for an outdoor event. There's nothing like a wedding candle that refuses to light or stay lit for a bride and groom just starting out — the truly inauspicious beginning.

2. **Know thy wedding planner.** Many wineries have a person on staff responsible for wedding planning or they can recommend someone, if you need one. My advice — embrace a planner's services. Bring her lattes and befriend her (or him, as the case may be). The fact is, these people have tons of experience and know the pitfalls that lead to not-so-wonderful weddings. They can suggest a caterer, photographer, florist, transportation service, wedding officiant, and more. You don't have to use a planner, but through personal experience, this person has identified the most reliable and highest-qualified companies in the area for these one-time services.

Weather can be unpredictable / Woodriver Cellars

Once you have met with a wedding planner, reconnect with her/him several months in advance of the ceremony and go through the myriad details associated with the event. By this time, you might have a special request that you didn't address the first time. For example, if you want champagne at each table for a toast, but the winery doesn't make sparkling wine, how do you handle that? Is it copacetic with the winery if you want to exchange vows while stomping grapes in a tub at harvest? **WineTrail Note:** Ina De Boer, the wedding and events planner for Idaho's Sawtooth Winery, recalled one couple who had their border collie serve as the ring bearer! On another occasion, a groom parachuted into the wedding — and lived to exchange vows with his bride. This is your special day, and it needs to reflect your personalities.

As the big day approaches, it is a good idea to visit the winery during the time of day you have reserved. Note the light and wind conditions. Review the other "little things" that you didn't think about earlier, such as:

- Does the bride's dressing room have full-length mirrors?
- Does the groom's area have flat-panel TV? (This may sound trivial, but ZenithVineyard in Oregon provides a dedicated space for grooms complete with DVDs for movie watching. Nice touch.)
- Will the musicians be positioned where they can be heard?
- Does the ceremonial area allow for wheelchair access?
- Will uninvited winery visitors be able to wander into the event à la Wedding Crashers?
- What happens in the event of bad weather? Is the inside space large enough to accommodate your party? Will you need to rent a tent as a backup?

3. **Expect the unexpected.** I understand that you think you have thought through all contingencies. But remember Murphy's Law: "Whatever can go wrong will go wrong," and be prepared for the unexpected. On the big day, emotions will be running high, and if the caterer should fail to deliver the ginger-peanut sauce for the fire-grilled, spiced chicken skewers, don't freak out. Life will go on and your guests won't mind. In fact, they might not even notice.

4. **Plan to arrive early.** This is the time to review and change the setup. If Aunt Bertha forgot the special guest book, you can call your best friend and ask her to stop by the mall and pick one up. If the power cord isn't long enough to reach the AV equipment, there's time to dash to ACE Hardware for a new one. No worries, mate. Just relax and realize that these things will happen and add to your special day. Friends of mine related that on their wedding day, their linens had been mixed up with those of a nearby hotel and they received form-fitting sheets for queen-size beds instead of regular tablecloths. After the bride's mother had a conniption, the groom and his friends draped the outdoor tables with the sheets, and after a few rounds of wine, the assembled crowd had a good laugh!

Now, one more piece of advice, which is probably the most important tip I can give: Have fun!

Ste. Chapelle Winery

Panhandle
WINE COUNTRY

North Idaho
Wine Trail

Lake Coeur d'Alene

Stretching from Sandpoint in the north to Lewiston in the south, the North Idaho Wine Trail offers a number of remarkable wine stops to experience — that's in addition to its sparkling lakes, rugged mountains, and destination resort towns. Working your way from north to south on U.S. Highway 95, you will visit four distinguished wineries. Pend d'Oreille Winery's location in the energetic town of Sandpoint is ideal for outdoor adventurers. If you are there in the winter, plan on *après-ski* wine tasting. If time and budget permit, book an overnight stay at Coeur d'Alene Resort and experience this quaint city, with its abundance of restaurants, art galleries, and parks. But first enjoy the gorgeous wines at Coeur d'Alene Cellars. The college town of Moscow is a fun stop, and Camas Prairie Winery's location in downtown Moscow may encourage Wine Trail trekkers to don their sneakers for brisk walk around the University of Idaho campus nearby. The final stop along this Wine Trail is historic Lewiston. This geologic wonderland was the site of nearly 100 acres of premium wine grapes in the early 1900s. However, there's no truth to the rumor that Lewis and Clark's Corps of Discovery stopped here to purchase cabernet sauvignon.

North Idaho WineTrail

1 Pend d'Oreille Winery
2 Coeur d'Alene Cellars
3 Camas Prairie Winery
4 Clearwater Canyon Cellars

95
95
2
1
Sandpoint
2
200
95
To Spokane
2
Coeur d'Alene
90
95
To Kellogg
95
3
Moscow
95
4
Clarkston

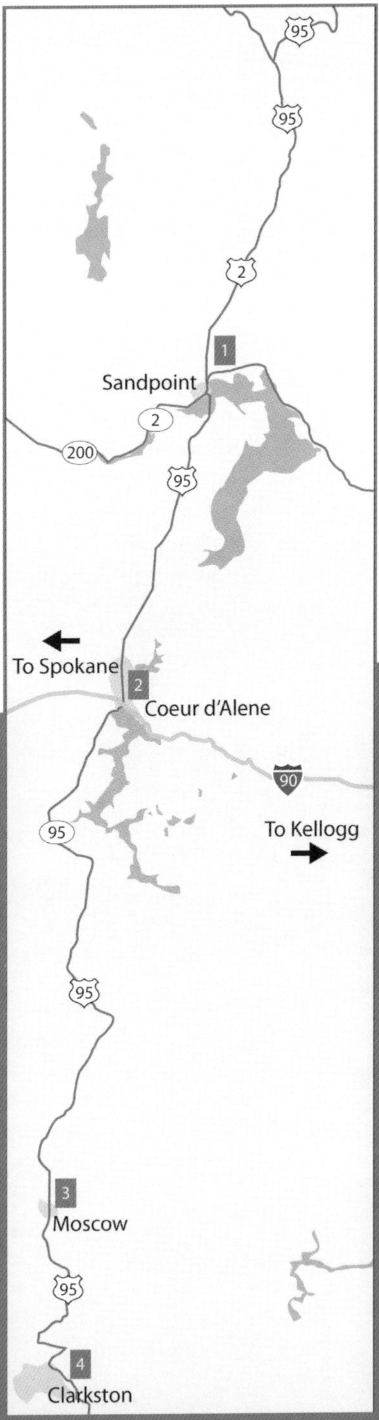

Region:	**Panhandle Wine Country**
# of tasting rooms on tour:	**4**
Estimate # of days for tour:	**2**
Getting around:	**Car, RV**

Events:

- ❑ **Check out www.winetrailsnw.com for a listing of key events.**
- ❑ **Pend d'Oreille Winery hosts Friday night live music concerts; see www.powine.com for event information.**

Tips:

- ❑ **Have a hankering for beer instead of wine? No problem at Camas Prairie Winery where dozens of hard-to-find imported beers await you.**
- ❑ **Coeur d'Alene Cellars Barrel Room No.6 in the Coeur d'Alene's downtown district is an upscale venue available to host special events.**

Pend d'Oreille Winery

A visit to the Pend d'Oreille Winery website had me scrambling for my French phrase book. On the home page is the maxim *"Rêves ta vie, vis tes rêves,"* meaning "Dream your life, live your dreams." The phrase struck a chord with owners Steve and Julie Meyer when they were gaining winemaking experience in France during the mid-'80s. It was there that they observed how wine is an important ingredient for the local lifestyle; not an end in itself, but rather, a beverage to be shared with friends, family, and a meal.

Located in the former Pend d'Oreille Brewery in downtown Sandpoint, the Pend d'Oreille Winery goes way beyond the concept of a simple tasting room. It holds a gift shop proffering elegant gifts for home, garden and life (such as natural bamboo dishtowels, *Pizza on the Grill* cookbook, and Riedel stemware), a handsome handcrafted concrete wine bar, and casual space for live music. For tasting wine, comfy bar stools invite guests to sit rather than stand.

Given Pend d'Oreille's wide assortment of whites, reds, and sweet wines (including a beguiling Huckleberry Blush), you may find yourself planted on that stool for a while. In between smelling the floral notes in my sample of pinot gris, I asked the pourer where Pend d'Oreille Winery gets its grapes. It turns out that its fruit comes from both Washington and Idaho growers. The fact is, logistically, it's a lot easier for a winery in Sandpoint to get grapes from Washington's premium Columbia Valley vineyards. As we moved on to the subject of the winery's award-winning reds, our conversation was interrupted when someone came in with an empty magnum bottle. What's this I wondered...

Adopting the slogan "Think green, drink red," Pend d'Oreille Winery began an innovative refillable-bottle program featuring its food-friendly Bistro Rouge red table wine. An innovative idea to us maybe, but refillable wine bottles are common practice in the French countryside. The first bottle costs $25, but after that, the magnums are refilled at a recession-busting $16. In Idaho's Panhandle, the refill program is a huge hit with many fans of Pend d'Oreille Winery, who refill their magnums two or three times a month!

Now I understand the Meyers' mantra "Dream your life, live your dreams." Steve and Julie are living the dream they envisioned years ago in the vineyards of France. To them I lift my glass and say, "Santé!"

PEND D'OREILLE WINERY
opened: 1995
winemaker(s): Julie and Stephen Meyer; James Bopp
location: 220 Cedar Street, Sandpoint, ID 83864
phone: 208-265-8545
web: www.powine.com
e-mail: info@powine.com
picnic area: Yes
wheelchair access: Yes
gift shop: Yes
tours: Yes
fee: Tasting fee applies
hours: Monday through Thursday 10–6:30;
Friday and Saturday 10–8; Sunday 11–6
lat: 48.276262 **long:** -116.549191

DIRECTIONS: From US 95 North/South, or Rt. 2 East, turn onto 1st Ave. and continue until it becomes Cedar St. Arrive at the winery (corner of 3rd and Cedar) and park in the winery parking lot, or anywhere on 3rd.

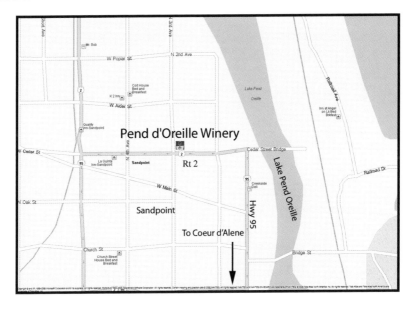

Coeur d'Alene Cellars ②

Hypothetically, if I could assume ownership of one Idaho winery, I would have to say that winery would be Coeur d'Alene Cellars. Why? I am a lover of syrah, and Coeur d'Alene Cellars is Idaho's mecca for Rhône varietal wines and in particular, syrah. But don't take my word for it — take that of *Wine Spectator*, which gave Coeur d'Alene Cellars' 2006 Envy Syrah and 2006 Boushey Vineyard Syrah scores of 90 and 92 points, respectively.

Typically when an enterprise is "under new management," changes abound. However, in my Coeur d'Alene ownership fantasy, I realize I wouldn't change a thing. The Gates

family, led by the young and energetic Kimber Gates, armed with a CPA background and strong business acumen, has created a winery consisting of a state-of-the-art facility, established relationships with premier Washington grape growers, and an experienced winemaker in Warren Schutz, a graduate of University of California, Davis' famed enology program. I'd even keep the labels adorning their bottles, which bear original watercolors painted by Kimber's mom, Sarah Gates. You may wonder what I would bring to the table, and the answer would be nada, zilch, zippo. Am I embarrassed? Not at all. Why muck up a good thing?

My Coeur d'Alene Cellars sojourn afforded me the opportunity to experience first-hand its contemporary production facility and tasting room. While I sampled the delightfully crisp 2007 L'Artiste Viognier (love the name… I wouldn't change that either), Kimber noted that they enjoy good working relationships with Columbia Valley growers. With vintage names such as McKinley Springs, Alder Ridge, Elephant Mountain and Boushey, it's clear that Coeur d'Alene Cellars sources its grapes from a who's who of the upper crust of Washington grape growers. She went on to say that it is easy for them logistically to acquire grapes, unlike their winemaking counterparts in western Washington, who have to deal with mountain passes.

My tour of the facility continued into the production and barrel room area, where cellar harvest master Brian Logan joined us. Like Kimber, Brian also attended Walla Walla's Whitman College, where he picked up a degree in chemistry. Surrounded by red-stained French oak barrels, I managed to take a few pictures while reflecting on the idea that these two people — young, energetic, full of promise, and poised to add their own unique signatures — truly embody the Idaho wine industry. That's not hypothesis; that's reality.

COEUR D'ALENE CELLARS
opened: 2002
winemaker(s): Warren Schutz
location: 3890 North Schreiber Way,
Coeur d'Alene, ID 83815
phone: 208-664-2336
web: www.cdacellars.com
e-mail: info@cdacellars.com
wheelchair access: Yes
fee: Small tasting fee applies
hours: Monday through Saturday 11–5
lat: 47.711817 **long:** -116.802733

Brian Logan and Kimber Gates

DIRECTIONS: Heading south on US-95 entering Coeur d'Alene turn right (west) onto W Kathleen Ave. and go .3 miles. Turn left (south) onto N Schreiber Way and arrive at winery on the left in .4 miles.

Heading east or west on I-90 and take exit 11. Go north onto N Ramsey Rd and go 1.1 miles. Turn right (east) onto W Kathleen Ave. and continue .3 miles. Turn right (south) onto N Schreiber Way, the winery will appear on the left in .4 miles.

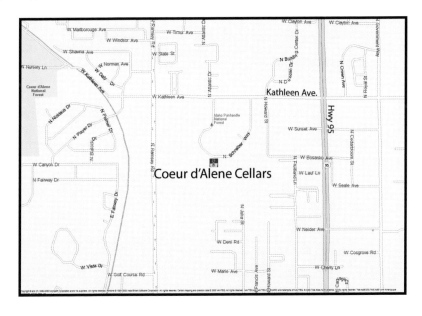

Camas Prairie Winery 3

"It's nice to be recognized," admitted a modest Stu Scott, owner and winemaker of Camas Prairie Winery. Stu was referring to the fact that in 2007, Wine Press Northwest named Camas Prairie Winery the Idaho Winery of the Year. A big contributing factor for this accolade is Camas Prairie Winery's knack for racking up "Best Buy" awards. With most prices in the teens, Camas Prairie wines are a good value. Even Stu's cabernet sauvignon checks in at less than $20 a bottle.

Stu and his wife, Sue, have had more than 20 years to fine-tune their winery business, and they understand how to survive in a difficult market. "Let's face it, Moscow, Idaho, is not exactly a wine destination," Stu noted. But as the owner of the oldest winery in northern Idaho (it acquired the title of Idaho Bonded Winery No. 15 in 1983), he understands

that "if you make what you like, that's a hobby, but if you make what the customers like, that's called a business." Thus, Camas Prairie Winery offers a variety of wines: In addition to premium table wines, it makes a full slate of slightly sweet wines (residual sugar between 2 percent and 4 percent), sweet dessert wines (a lip-smacking 8.5 percent and 12 percent residual sugar), plum wines and honey wines. Stu even makes sparkling wines using the traditional méthode Champenoise technique. **WineTrail Note:** If someone in your touring group has a hankering for beer rather than wine, no worries! Camas Prairie Winery has on hand the largest selection of European bottled beers in northern Idaho.

Camas Prairie Winery is a case study in efficiency. Everything about the winery — the use of space, the makeshift equipment it relies upon, and even the implementation of rooftop solar panels speaks to efficiency. Stu, a past guest speaker at the University of Idaho's entrepreneurship program, understands the production costs associated with making and selling wine. For example, by making plum and mead wines, he is able to use his equipment during non-harvest times. And by selling more than 70 percent of his wines at the tasting room, he can make a modest profit. Even his living quarters are nearby — upstairs, as a matter of fact. (I figure that Stu and Sue's commute time is roughly 22 seconds.) It's little wonder that he can sell wines at such remarkable prices. I didn't blink when purchasing a $12 bottle of Ewe Eye White (gewürztraminer). Cheers!

www.winetrailsnw.com/wineries/camas_prairie_winery

CAMAS PRAIRIE WINERY
opened: 1983
winemaker(s): Stuart Scott
location: 110 South Main Street, Moscow, ID 83843
phone: 208-882-0214
web: www.camasprairiewinery.com
e-mail: scottcamas@turbonet.com
gift shop: Yes
fee: Small tasting fee
hours: Monday through Saturday 12–6:30
lat: 46.733562 **long:** -117.001287

DIRECTIONS: Entering Moscow from the north on Hwy 95 turn right (west) onto US-95 [W D St.], turn left south onto US-95 [N Jackson St.] and go .3 miles. Turn left (east) onto W 1st St. and continue to 110 S Main St.

Heading north on US-95 from Lewiston turn left (west) onto SR-8 [E 3rd St.], then immediately right (north) onto S Main St. and arrive at tasting room.

From Pullman, take SR-270 about 9 miles to Moscow. Road name changes to SR-8 when entering Idaho. Turn left (north) onto S Main St. and arrive at 110 S Main St.

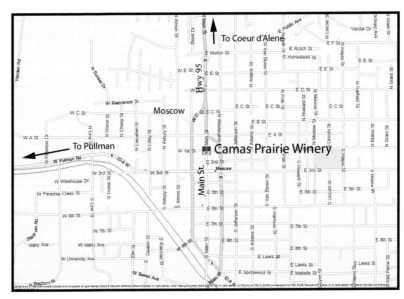

Clearwater Canyon Cellars 4

"It may not be too visionary to dream of the slopes and hillsides of the Snake and Clearwater rivers being covered with vineyards." These are the words of award-winning vintner Robert Schleicher in 1906 when the Clearwater Canyon area was emerging as premium wine grape country. Then Prohibition came, and the fledging wine industry died a quick death.

Umiker Vineyard

Thus, it seems only fitting that in 2005, Clearwater Canyon Cellars released its first vintage under the name Renaissance Red. Eight Lewiston-based people — Coco and Karl Umiker, Gary Rencehausen and his spouse, Barb Nedrow, Joann Cole-Hansen and her spouse, Jerome Hansen, and Patty and Tim Switzer — came together to form the winery after attending a grape-growing class in nearby Clarkston. Like a Bordeaux blend, the winery is a result of the fine mix of each person's set of skills and experiences. However, for the actual winemaking, the group relies on Coco. Despite her 20-something youth, she possesses considerable experience in winemaking from a stint in Walla Walla as well as an advanced degree in winemaking from Washington State University.

In time, the Clearwater Canyon area may become a designated American viticultural area. Starting out in 2004 the winery had to rely in large part upon grapes from Washington's Horse Heaven Hills AVA and other Columbia Valley vineyards. However, with each vintage, an increasing percentage of the grapes are locally grown and now compose approximately 85% of Clearwater Canyon's total production. As Patty Switzer pointed out, "Our goal is to use local fruit. Increasingly, our grapes will come from growers here in the Lewiston Clarkston Valley."

During my visit to the winery, Patty, with thief and wine glass in hand, created a blend of locally sourced syrah and merlot for my tasting pleasure. As I stuck my nose into the wine glass and took a whiff, I couldn't help but think of how those early winemaking pioneers would have slapped high fives at seeing the reemergence of the Idaho wine industry in the Clearwater Canyon area. It's clear that Clearwater Canyon Cellars honors the past but looks resolutely to a bright future

Currently, the winery is only open to the public on Saturdays from October through December. This is due in large part to fact that the winery sells out of its limited supply. As my dad would say, "That's a good problem." At 600 cases per year, there's only so much wine to go around!

www.winetrailsnw.com/wineries/clearwater_canyon_cellars

CLEARWATER CANYON CELLARS
opened: 2004
winemaker(s): Coco Umiker
location: 1708 6th Avenue North, Suite A,
Lewiston, ID 83501
phone: 208-816-4679
web: www.cccellars.com
e-mail: switzer@cccellars.com
fee: Complimentary wine tasting
hours: Saturday 1–5 October through December
or by appointment
lat: 46.426434 **long:** -117.00828

Co-owner and winemaker Coco Umiker

DIRECTIONS: Heading south on US-95 from Moscow take ramp onto US-12 and proceed .8 miles toward US-12 / Lewiston / Walla Walla. Keep right onto Freeway Bypass and go .2 miles. Turn left (southwest) onto 20th St. N, then immediately bear right (west) onto 6th Ave. N. Arrive at 1708 6th Ave. N, Suite A.

From Lewiston, take US-12 [Main St.] east 1.5 miles. Bear left onto SR-128 [Down River Rd] and go .2 miles. Turn left onto 20th St. N, then bear right (west) onto 6th Ave. N and go .2 miles to arrive at winery.

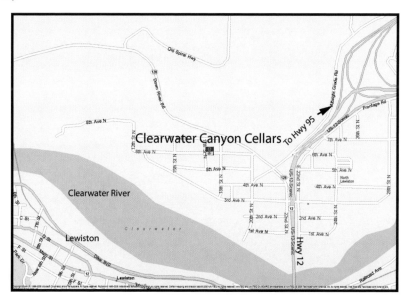

Snake River West
WINE COUNTRY

Sunnyslope
Wine Trail

Hells Canyon Winery

OK, if you have limited time and can't hit all Idaho wineries, here's a **WineTrail Tip:** Tour the Sunnyslope WineTrail. Nearby Boise offers plenty of great places to stay with easy access to this agriculture heartland. With the Snake River meandering its way for hundreds of miles through it, the Sunnyslope area is a patchwork quilt of farms, with potato fields, fruit orchards and well-groomed vineyards. Here you'll find the state's oldest wineries and vineyards, including its biggest winery, Ste. Chapelle Winery, and a wide array of red and white wines using (for the most part) premium grapes from the Snake River Valley AVA. With rolling hills aplenty, you can opt to bring your bike along for some guaranteed aerobic workouts. If hunger pangs hit after all that swirling and sipping, check out the Orchard House Restaurant (located within spitting distance of Koenig Distillery & Winery and Williamson Orchards & Vineyards), or for some good ol' home cooking, eat at Brick 29 Bistro in Nampa. Both feature locally grown foods and wines from the Sunnyslope WineTrail wineries.

Sunnyslope WineTrail

1. Fujishin Family Cellars
2. Bitner Vineyards
3. Koenig Distillery & Winery
4. Williamson Orchards & Vineyards
5. Ste. Chapelle Winery
6. Hells Canyon Winery
7. Davis Creek Cellars
8. Sawtooth Winery

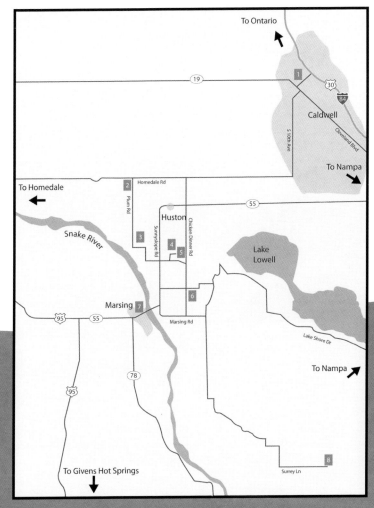

Region:	**Snake River Wine Country West**
# of tasting rooms on tour:	**8**
Estimate # of days for tour:	**2**
Getting around:	**Car and bicycle**

Tips:
- ❑ **Good eats: Orchard House Restaurant in Caldwell; Brick 29 Bistro in Nampa; or Sandbar River House in Marsing**
- ❑ **Don't forget cooler in summer — you don't want to cook your purchased wine in summer's heat**
- ❑ **If you visit in the fall, be sure and check out Williamson Orchard & Vineyard's fruit stand**
- ❑ **Need a place to get married? Consider Ste. Chapelle Winery or Sawtooth Winery's spacious grounds**

Fujishin Family Cellars 1

"Eighteen degrees brix," exclaimed Martin Fujishin after popping a syrah grape in his mouth. It was late August, and his gleeful smile said it all: Harvest was just around the corner. We were standing between one of many well-pruned rows of the 110-acre Bitner Vineyards, which Martin manages. He was giving me a two-minute viticulture drill on canopy management, and it was clear he cares about every vine.

Given Martin's callused hands and deep viticultural understanding, I believe he will make a fine instructor at the fledging Treasure Valley Community College viticulture program, where he began teaching in the fall of 2009. Of course, I had to ask, "Would you want

Martin Fujishin

to have your own vineyard?" "Oh, heck no," was his quick response. "There's no time for that. I work five jobs!"

Martin beat me to the punch before I could inquire about those five jobs, He explained that he also works part-time for the Idaho Department of Agriculture, spending a couple of days a week inspecting vineyards in the Snake River AVA. Such work brings him in close contact with other wine growers, with whom conversations about mildew and mealy bugs might leave other mortals yawning, but not Martin.

He's also the assistant winemaker at Koenig Distillery & Winery, where for several years now, Martin has learned first-hand from one of Idaho's premier winemakers, Greg Koenig. This experience has informed him in the craft of winemaking and shaped his winemaking style — a style that relies more on art than science, as well as on trust in his own palate. It has also taught him that winemaking is just half the battle of running a successful winery. The other half is marketing. Fortunately for Martin, his girlfriend and business partner, Teresa Moye, takes on the all-important role of marketing person and tasting-room coordinator for Fujishin Family Cellars.

In Caldwell's Urban Renewal District, at Fujishin's new tasting room, dubbed Coyotes, visitors can sample Martin's wines, poured from bottles adorned with his family crest. For those with a penchant for Rhône-style wines — syrah and viognier — you are in luck. These are Martin's favorites, and his description of viognier's "bright floral notes" had me drooling.

Vineyard manager, winemaker, winery owner, agriculture inspector, college instructor — how's that for a résumé? I was exhausted just contemplating this human version of the Energizer bunny. But with apologies to Robert Frost, at 30 years of age, Martin has many vintages to go before he sleeps.

www.winetrailsnw.com/wineries/fujishin_family_cellars

Martin Fujishin

FUJISHIN FAMILY CELLARS
opened: 2009
winemaker(s): Martin Fujishin
location: 217 South Kimball, Caldwell, ID 83605
phone: 208-573-0793
web: www.fujishinfamilycellars.com
e-mail: info@fujishinfamilycellars.com
fee: Tasting fee may apply
hours: TBD
lat: 43.6654996 **long:** -116.6882081

DIRECTIONS: Heading east or west on I-84, take exit 28 toward Caldwell. Turn left (south) onto 10th Ave. and keep straight for .5 miles. Hang a right onto Arthur St. and arrive at 217 S Kimball Ave.

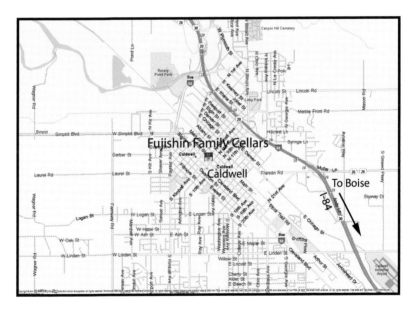

Bitner Vineyards 2

With a youthful smile, graying hair and engaging eyes, 62-year-old Ron Bitner welcomed me to his vineyard and winery (as did his Jack Russell terriers, Jimmie and Brix, circling my feet with tails wagging in perpetual motion). With nearly 30 years in the grape-growing and wine-making profession, Ron knows a thing or two about wine making. However, he wasn't always so informed. Back in 1980, when he bought the property, a grape grower suggested that he plant chardonnay. Ron's reaction? "What's chardonnay?" he asked.

Since their first *Vitis vinifera* plantings in the early '80s, Ron and his wife, Mary, have nurtured the vineyard and expanded it to 16 acres of chardonnay, riesling, cabernet sauvignon, merlot, petit verdot and syrah (which Ron refers to as shiraz, a holdover from his frequent forays to Australia over the years). At first, the Bitners' goal was to grow first-class grapes expressing the *terroir* of the Snake River Valley. However, that goal morphed into grape growing *and* wine making when they engaged the wine-making services of their neighbor Greg Koenig of Koenig Winery & Distillery in 1995. Since then, the accolades and awards have mounted. Note the fact that Bitner Vineyards was honored with the title of 2009 *Wine Press Northwest* Idaho Winery of the Year. That's not bad for a couple who once found themselves wondering what to do with a hillside full of tumbleweeds.

The Bitners' Mediterranean-hued tasting room offers a friendly space to sample wine and choose a favorite to enjoy on the generous deck outside. In the June sun, the rows of emerald vineyards gave way to the bountiful valley and the Snake River, with the Owyhee Mountains in the distance. The scenery is quintessential southern Idaho and truly defines Canyon County.

While snapping pictures during my visit, I asked Ron about the bee on the Bitner logo. "I'm a bee biologist," he confided and went on to explain that he earned his doctorate in entomology at Utah State University. In fact, his doctoral thesis has the page-turning title "Ecological Management of the Alfalfa Leafcutting Bee, *Megachile rotundata*." His interest in bees would explain 24 separate trips to Australia over the past 10 years to consult on bee-related projects. As educational as his thesis surely is, this WineTrail trekker will forgo reading it and make a beeline for a bottle of Bitner Vineyards Reserve Cabernet Sauvignon instead.

Ron Bitner

BITNER VINEYARDS
opened: 1985
winemaker(s): Greg Koenig
location: 16645 Plum Road, Caldwell, ID 83607
phone: 208-899-7648
web: www.bitnervineyards.com
e-mail: bitner.wines@bitnervineyards.com
picnic area: Yes
wheelchair access: Yes
fee: Tasting fee may apply
hours: Friday through Sunday 12–5 or by appointment
lat: 43.612114 **long:** -116.81273

DIRECTIONS: Going west from Boise on I-84, take exit 35 toward ID-55 (Nampa Blvd / Marsing) and go right (north) onto Northside Blvd .2 miles. Turn left (west) onto W Karcher Rd and proceed 1.5 miles. Road name changes to SR-55 [W Karcher Rd] and continue for 9.5 miles. Hang a right onto Hoskins Rd and go 1.1 miles. Turn right onto Plum Rd and arrive at winery.

Heading east on I-84 toward Caldwell, take exit 28 and go south on 10th Ave. to Hwy 55 (Karcher Rd) and turn right. Once on Hwy 55, go west and veer right on Hoskins Rd and right again on Plum Rd. Go up and over the hill and look for "Bitner Vineyards" sign.

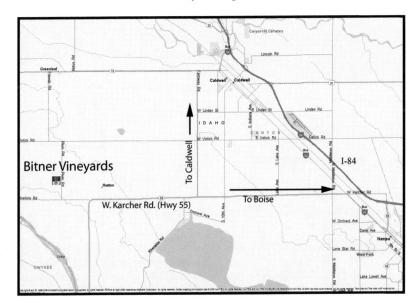

Koenig Distillery & Winery ❸

Brothers Andrew and Greg Koenig have something special going on in the Sunnyslope area of southwest Idaho. It may look like a "little slice of heaven," but don't think for a moment that it was the result of dumb luck or winning the lottery. Rather, transforming a 72-acre farm — complete with orchards, premium wine grapes, and potatoes — takes hard work, drive and a healthy dose of family history. It was a three-year stint in their father's Austrian hometown that taught them the art of distillation and creating brandies from fine fruit. Eventually, when the brothers began producing distilled spirits and wine,

it just seemed right to use a family-style coat of arms for the image on their bottle labels — a nice touch.

WineTrail fans may find themselves starting to salivate when they turn onto Grape Lane and drive the short distance to Koenig Distillery & Winery. There, surrounded by fruit trees and rich farmland, is the classically styled two-story, honey-colored production facility and tasting room. It turns out that Greg is an architect, having honed his skills at the University of Notre Dame. He designed the facility and had the insight to house the tasting room on the upper floor, where the outside deck provides a commanding view of the Snake River Valley.

Once you sample Greg's delectable lineup of wines — chardonnay, viognier, pinot noir, merlot, syrah, cabernet sauvignon, and Bordeaux blends — you begin to appreciate why Bitner Vineyards, Williamson Orchards & Vineyards, and 3 Horse Ranch Vineyards turn to him for his winemaking prowess. Greg's wines are truly remarkable, and I was most impressed by the Syrah Three Vineyard Cuvée, which displays blackberry and pepper flavors. But all his wines are yummy and showcase the unique flavor profiles of the Snake River AVA.

While you're in the tasting room, be sure to check out Andy's brandies and vodka. Small wonder that the potato state of Idaho would have a premium vodka distillery. His portfolio of brandies (aka *eaux-de-vie*) consists of single-fruit cherry, apricot, plum, pear, raspberry, and apple, as well as grappa (a grape brandy made from fermented pomace).

Brothers who share childhood memories can often go on to share grown-up dreams. In the case of Koenig Distillery & Winery, the Koenig brothers' dreams are reflected in the liquid of each bottle, as are their passion and love of southwest Idaho's bounty and their unabashed caring for one other.

Greg Koenig

KOENIG DISTILLERY & WINERY
winemaker(s): Andrew and Greg Koenig
location: 20928 Grape Lane, Caldwell, ID 83605
phone: 208-455-8386
web: www.koenigdistillery.com
e-mail: info@koenigvineyards.com
picnic area: Yes
fee: Tasting fee may apply
hours: Saturday and Sunday 12–5 or by appointment
lat: 43.581531 **long:** -116.810307

DIRECTIONS: From I-84 heading east or west, take exit 33 [Nampa / Marsing] to SR-55 [W Karcher Rd] and drive about 10 miles towards Marsing. In the Sunny Slope area, turn right (west) onto Pear Ln. and go .5 miles. Go left (south) onto Frost Rd and continue 1 mile. Turn right (west) onto Grape Ln. and find the winery at 20928 Grape Ln.

Williamson Orchards & Vineyards 4

"I'm the wine grower," remarked 60-something Roger Williamson. Sporting a neatly cropped beard and winning smile, Roger knows his place in the family business. Everyone seems to have a unique role at Williamson Orchards & Vineyards, where Roger and his brother John oversee the 700-acre farm, which produces row crops and fruit, including premium wine grapes. Roger's daughter Beverly smiled and agreed that each family member has an integral part in the operation. She is in charge of sales and marketing. Roger's son Michael manages the vineyard. "Even my nephew Patrick is going to Walla

Walla Community College to get a degree in enology to learn about winemaking," noted Roger.

Growing premium grapes is one thing, but you need an experienced winemaker to turn grapes into wine. Fortunately for the Williamsons, their nearby neighbor happens to be one of the most sought-after winemakers in Idaho: Greg Koenig. The relationship is symbiotic. Greg gets much of his fruit from Williamson vineyards, and the Williamsons get about 1,000 cases of award-winning wines in return. As a testament to just how good the Williamsons' fruit is, it is used to make Koenig Distillery & Winery's most expensive bottle of wine, which also happens to be the most expensive bottle of Idaho wine on the market. At a mere $50 a bottle, you can be the first kid on the block to own a 2005 Cuvee Amelia Reserve.

Although the Williamsons grow more than just wine grapes, the popularity of those grapes with a number of local wineries (each of which secured long-term contracts for the fruit) led Roger and John to branch out and produce their own wine. You can bet that, from the 38 acres under grape production, the Williamsons reserve the best grapes for their own label. At the Williamson tasting room, WineTrail trekkers can taste riesling, viognier, cabernet sauvignon, syrah, and dessert-style wines, all made from estate grapes.

The Williamson fruit stand and tasting room are open June through December. It's one of the few places where you can find cherries, pears, nectarines and apples alongside cabernet sauvignon. However, product availability varies week to week, and it's a good idea to call ahead to find out what's being offered. As the Williamsons say on their website, "Keep in mind, Mother Nature is the one in charge, and we pick by her schedule."

WILLIAMSON ORCHARDS & VINEYARDS
winemaker(s): Greg Koenig
location: 19692 Williamson Lane, Caldwell, ID 83605
phone: 208-459-7333
web: www.willorch.com
e-mail: wine@willorch.com
picnic area: Yes
gift shop: Yes
fee: Small tasting fee for reserve cab; refundable with purchase
hours: Monday through Friday 10–6 and Saturday and Sunday 10–4, from June through December; Off Season – by appointment only
lat: 43.576952 **long:** -116.792161

DIRECTIONS: If heading west on I-84 from Oregon border, take exit 27 toward ID-19 / Caldwell / Homedale. Turn right (west) onto I-84 Bus [SR-19] and go .8 miles. Veer right (west) onto SR-19 [E Simplot Blvd.] and go .8 miles. Turn left (south) onto Farmway Rd and continue 4.5 miles. Hang a right (west) onto SR-55 [W ID-55] and go 5.7 miles to arrive at 19692 Williamson Ln.

From Boise, take I-84 west heading towards Nampa/Caldwell. Get off the interstate at the Karcher Interchange, exit 33A. This will direct you onto Hwy 55 [Karcher Rd]. Look for signs for Marsing to make sure you are in the correct lane. Follow Hwy 55 for approximately 15 miles and look for Williamson Vineyard sign on the left hand side of the road. Turn left on Williamson Ln. The fruit stand and the winery are in between the packing shed and the house.

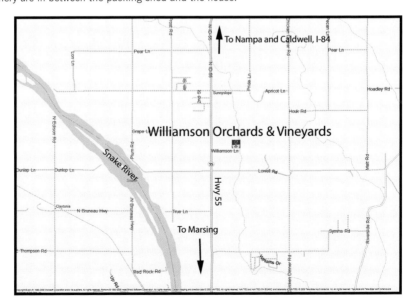

Ste. Chapelle Winery 5

When it comes to the Idaho wine industry, Ste. Chapelle Winery is its 800-pound gorilla — and for good reason. Founded in 1976 and producing 160,000 cases annually, Ste. Chapelle Winery is the oldest and largest winery in Idaho. In fact, the total production of all other Gem State wineries combined is only 55 percent of Ste. Chapelle's output. As my Grandfather Talcott would say, "Every good shopping mall needs a Nordstrom as a tenant." Truly, Ste. Chapelle Winery is that anchor for Idaho's wine industry.

Open wrought-iron gates welcome visitors to enter Ste. Chapelle Winery. In the distance is the winery's French-inspired tasting room sitting atop the aptly named Winery Hill. Here in the high-desert area of Sunnyslope, you can look down upon the valley floor and

see thousands of acres of rich farmland, with the Snake River meandering in the distance.

With its vaulted ceilings with wooden beams and a stained-glass grapevine window, the tasting room reflects the Gothic features of the Sainte-Chapelle in Paris. It gives visitors a sense of weightlessness, which was clearly one of the design goals of the King Louis IX's architects in the 13th century, when they built that chapel. However, don't expect robed monks greeting visitors and talking up the virtues of riesling. Rather, for a small fee, the friendly, well-trained tasting-room staff will lead you through a robust lineup of delectable wines. Singing their praises is optional.

Visitors can experience winemaker Chuck Devlin's many creations by beginning with riesling (which really put Ste. Chapelle Winery on the proverbial map) and moving on to other whites, including barrel-aged chardonnay, sauvignon blanc, and gewürztraminer The reds featured are Rhône- and Bordeaux-style wines, but be sure to save room for Ste. Chapelle's top seller, Soft Red. With 35,000 cases produced annually, Soft Red is easily Idaho's number-one-selling wine. Note that this wine checks in at a hefty 6.5 percent residual sugar. It's like a dessert wine in drag.

Ste. Chapelle is a destination winery. Pack a picnic; with the winery's ample grounds and beautiful views, visitors can easily swirl, sip and nosh their way through an afternoon. WineTrail trekkers can maximize their visit by calling ahead and arranging a tour of the production facility. However, to turbo-charge your stay, schedule your visit to coincide with Ste. Chapelle's popular summer concert series (see www.stechapelle.com for event information). Just remember to bring a corkscrew.

STE. CHAPELLE WINERY
opened: 1976
winemaker(s): Chuck Devlin
location: 19348 Lowell Road, Caldwell, ID 83607
phone: 208-453-7843
web: www.stechapelle.com
e-mail: tastingroom@stechapelle.com
picnic area: Yes
weddings: Yes
gift shop: Yes
tours: Yes
fee: Tasting fee waived for wine club members
hours: Monday through Saturday 10–5; Sunday 12–5
lat: 43.573781 **long:** -116.778820

DIRECTIONS: **From Ontario, OR** take I-84 east to exit 28 toward 10th Avenue. Turn right and go 5 miles to Hwy 55 and turn right. Drive another 7.5 miles to Ste. Chapelle's second road sign and turn left on Lowell Road. Proceed .75 miles veer left into the winery.

From Boise take I-84 west to exit 33A — towards Nampa/Marsing. At stop light continue straight onto Karcher Rd, which turns into Hwy 55. Go 12 miles to Lowell Road and turn left. Continue .75 of a mile and turn left into the winery.

From Caldwell take 10th Ave going south. Go to Hwy 55 and turn right going west. Travel 7 miles to Lowell Road and turn left. Continue .75 of a mile and veer left into the winery.

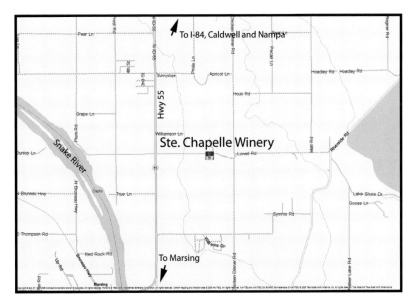

Hells Canyon Winery 6

"I wish them all the luck," said Steve Robertson referring to second-career winemakers jumping onto the winemaking bandwagon. However, it was Steve himself who, 25 years earlier, sold his highly successful restaurant in Boise to launch what would eventually become Hells Canyon Winery. Those wheels were set in motion when he found a plot of land off Chicken Dinner Road in Caldwell with a magnificent view of the Owyhee Mountains. But it was not by accident that Steve came to be a pioneer in the fledging Idaho wine industry. As a graduate of the Culinary Institute of America, Steve knew that

wine is a fine complement to food and part of a lifestyle he desired. He'd also possessed a healthy dose of wine making knowledge through his wine-related studies and traveling experience to guide him.

Today, Steve and his wife, Leslie, can boast that their 40-acre estate is the oldest vineyard in Idaho. From bud break to harvest and crush, Steve manages the process and produces estate wines of chardonnay, cabernet sauvignon, merlot, cabernet franc, and syrah. Admittedly, I'm a sucker for a pretty wine label. In the case of Hells Canyon Winery, the Artist Conservation Series labels, featuring original artwork of Idaho's game and wildlife, are impressive enough to make Eddie Bauer spring for his wallet.

Speaking of wine labels, I couldn't help but notice the brightly colored, slightly racy Zhoo Zhoo wine labels while sampling wine at the winery's chic Swallow's Wine Bar. Seeing my interest, Leslie explained that the Zhoo Zhoo wines are the creation of their three daughters: Bijou, Hadley, and Jocelyn. Following her father's example, Bijou Robertson is the assistant winemaker for Hells Canyon Winery and the winemaker for the Zhoo Zhoo line. Like her dad, Bijou also graduated from the Culinary Institute of America. The artwork that adorns the wine labels is the work of local artist Babette Beatty, and a number of her demurely *risqué* paintings grace the walls of the wine bar. For more information, see www.zhoozhoo.com.

After 25 years of living through the good times and the bad, Steve and Leslie Robertson have more than met the challenge of establishing a winery. They have carved out their own slice of heaven — a beautiful estate, luscious wine, and three striking daughters. As their motto succinctly puts it, "Come hell or high water, still out West!"

Steve and Leslie Robertson

HELLS CANYON WINERY
opened: 1980
winemaker(s): Steve Robertson and Assistant Winemaker Bijou Robertson
location: 18835 Symms Road, Caldwell, ID 83607
phone: 208-454-3300
web: www.hellscanyonwinery.org
e-mail: hellwine@yahoo.com
fee: Small tasting fee applies
hours: Swallows Wine Bar open Saturday and Sunday 12–5, but call ahead; Closed December through March
lat: 43.559553 **long:** -116.768955

DIRECTIONS: Take I-84 to exit 35 and follow signs for Hwy 55 south. Go about 13 miles from I-84, turn left on Riverside (Harvey's Fruit Stand) and continue on Riverside for 4 miles veering to the left after the dam and turn right at Symms Rd. Hells Canyon Winery is 1.5 miles on the left at 18835 Symms Rd.

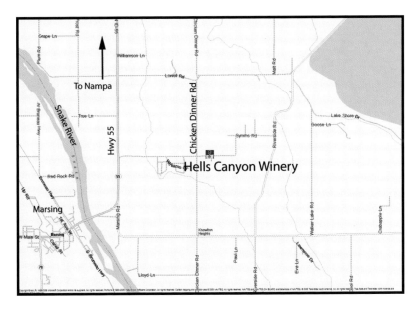

Davis Creek Cellars 7

Gina Davis, winemaker extraordinaire and owner of Davis Creek Cellars, is among the growing ranks of female winemakers in the Northwest. Referred to by some as a "wine diva," whatever reputation Gina enjoys has been earned through hard work and a healthy dose of experience.

A graduate of the University of Idaho with a degree in horticulture and crop science (she comes from a farming pedigree), Gina apprenticed at Ste. Chapelle Winery, Sawtooth Winery, and then Koenig Distillery & Vineyards before venturing out on her own. Not

only has she worked for renowned winemakers Brad Pintler (Sawtooth Winery) and Greg Koenig (Koenig Distillery & Vineyards), but she's also been exposed to the best of the best in terms of grape growers.

This in-depth knowledge of Idaho's grape growers allows Gina to choose the source of her fruit. She's not tied to a specific vineyard. She can get tempranillo from one grower and Malbec from another. What's more, if one grower suffers crop freeze, she can turn to another source for grapes. Although most growers she buys from are located in the Snake River Valley (e.g., Skyline Vineyards, Williamson Orchards, Woodriver Vineyards), she has also struck a deal with Scott Pontin of Pontin del Roza Vineyards in Prosser, Washington, to purchase his grapes.

Davis Creek Cellars' Marsing-based tasting room is located on the highway that leads through town, crossing the bridge over the Snake River. Housed in what was once the Owyhee Theater, the tasting room is *the* spot for sampling Gina's chardonnay, pinot grigio, riesling, viognier, cabernet sauvignon, Malbec, merlot, red blends, syrah and my personal favorite, tempranillo. The smell of theater popcorn has been replaced by the redolent smells of red wine. Here you can talk with Gina one on one or with her parents, George and Gayle Davis, who often help in the tasting room. Such intimacy is the advantage of small wineries.

With my nose stuck deep in a glass of syrah, I suddenly experienced a spine-tingling sense of exhilaration and reassurance — the Idaho wine industry is alive and well, thanks to people like Gina Davis. The future is rosé!

DAVIS CREEK CELLARS
winemaker(s): Gina Davis
location: 429 Main Street, Suite 101, PO Box 442, Marsing, ID 83639
phone: 208-794-2848
web: www.daviscreekcellars.com
e-mail: info@daviscreekcellars.com
gift shop: Yes
fee: Complimentary wine tasting
hours: Friday, Saturday, and Sunday from 12–5
lat: 43.544992 **long:** -116.809701

At downtown Boise farmer's market

DIRECTIONS: Traveling on I-84, take exit 33A to Hwy 55 (Karcher Rd). Go west to Marsing about 14 miles and arrive at 429 W Main St. across from US Bank in the Marsing Owyhee Plaza.

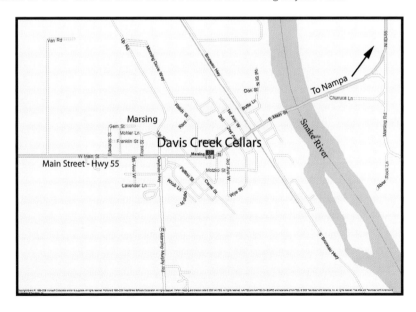

Sawtooth Winery 8

Sawtooth Winery is one of my favorite places to visit, hang out and savor the wine. Without further ado, I present my "Top Ten Reasons to Visit Sawtooth Winery," David Letterman style:

10. **Ample parking** — Whether there are tour buses or Memorial Day weekend visitors to contend with, parking is not an issue here. RV owners are welcomed.

9. **Well-heeled parent** — Seattle-based Corus Estates & Vineyards is the parent company of Sawtooth Winery. Providing more than deep pockets, it also brings a big-picture vision, marketing clout, and a focus on quality.

Bill Murray

8. **Supersized wine club** — Membership has its privileges and this is especially true with Sawtooth Winery's wine club. Besides Sawtooth Winery's goodies, club members have discounted access to Alder Ridge, Battle Creek, Zephina, and Six Prong wines.

7. **Labels** — The Sawtooth range provides the perfect imagery for these labels, but so do the other label images of the fly fisherman, trout and lure. They're quintessential Idaho.

6. **Panoramic views** — Clearly one of the best winery views in Idaho, hands down. From the hillside, you have acre upon acre of neatly cropped vineyards giving way to the Owyhee Mountains in the distance.

5. **Friendly staff** — Staff members welcome you with genuine smiles. It's obvious that they care.

4. **Ideal wedding venue** — If you desire an outdoor wedding, complete with beautiful gardens, a gazebo for photo ops, and plenty of space for dancing and dining, Sawtooth Winery fits the bill.

3. **Varietal smorgasbord** — Sawtooth's Estate Vineyard and sweeping Skyline Vineyard provide the fruit for a dozen different wines, from dry whites to rich Bordeaux-style reds, as well as dessert wines.

2. **Great prices** — With Sawtooth's estate cabernet sauvignon going for $16.99 a bottle, WineTrail trekkers will need plenty of space in the trunk for storing a case or two.

1. **Winemaker on a mission** — California transplant Bill Murray brings new energy and loads of winemaking experience and training for taking Sawtooth Winery to the next level.

Other WineTrail trekkers will discover their own top ten reasons why Idaho's second-largest winery (at 20,000 cases produced annually) continues to charm even the most jaded wine tourist. Sawtooth has hit upon the perfect formula for creating a truly memorable and uniquely Idahoan winery experience.

SAWTOOTH WINERY
opened: 1987
winemaker(s): Bill Murray
location: 13750 Surrey Lane, Nampa, ID 83686
phone: 208-467-1200
web: www.sawtoothwinery.com
e-mail: ideboer@sawtoothwinery.com
picnic area: Yes
weddings: Yes
gift shop: Yes
tours: Yes
fee: Tasting fee may apply
hours: Friday through Sunday 12–5
lat: 43.466462 **long:** -116.677898

DIRECTIONS: The winery is located about 10 miles south of Nampa on the hilltop overlooking Hidden Valley. **On I-84 go south** at exit 36 (Franklin exit) to 11th Ave. N and turn right to 3rd Street S. Turn left, 1 block to 12 Ave. S (Hwy 45) and turn right. Go 8 miles to Missouri Ave., turn right, and follow signs to the winery.

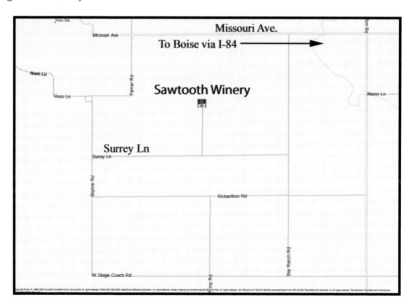

Boise Area
WineTrail

With beautiful Boise as their base camp, Boise Area WineTrail trekkers will experience a variety of settings — and wines — at four fabulous wineries. Beginning in Eagle's undulating countryside, the Boise Area WineTrail begins with a visit to 3 Horse Ranch Vineyards winery, which features organically grown fruit. With its rustic setting, it offers a safe haven for cowboys to drink viognier with their Brie and crackers. Down the road is the Woodriver Cellars estate. You will want to pack a picnic for this oasis. Bocce balls are optional. Next up is urban splendor in the chic BoDo district of Boise. You won't find vineyards here, but you will find plenty of tasty wines to sample at the Snake River Winery tasting room. Your final stop along this WineTrail is the bucolic Indian Creek Winery. By now, you will have had your fill of Bordeaux- and Rhône-style wines, but let's hope you've saved room for Indian Creek's pinot noir. There's a reason those bottles in Indian Creek's tasting room are draped in ribbons.

Boise Area WineTrail

1. 3 Horse Ranch Vineyards
2. Woodriver Cellars
3. Snake River Winery
4. Indian Creek Winery

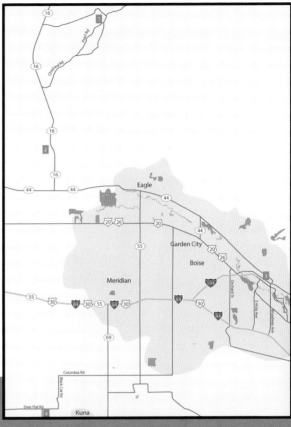

Region: **Snake River Wine Country West**

\# of tasting rooms on tour: **4**

Estimate # of days for tour: **1 or 2 days**

Getting around: **Car**

Tips: **Great eats in Boise:**
- ❑ Cafe Vicino, 888 W Fort Street, (208) 472-4500
- ❑ Red Feather Lounge, 246 North 8th Street, (208) 429-6340
- ❑ Andrea's Restaurant, 816 West Bannock, (208) 385-0707
- ❑ Bardenay Restaurant Distillery, 610 West Grove Street, (208) 426-0538
- ❑ Mortimer's 110 South 5th Street, (208) 338-6550

Lodging splurge:
- ❑ Hotel 43, 981 West Grove Street, (208) 342-4622
- ❑ The Grove Hotel, 245 Sout Capitol Blvd, (208) 333-8000

Museum trip:
- ❑ The Old Idaho Territorial Penitentiary, 2445 Old Penitentiary Road, Boise, ID 83712

Calorie burner:
- ❑ For walkers, runners and bicyclists check out 25-mile Boise River Greenbelt

3 Horse Ranch Vineyards

I was a little worried that I had taken a wrong turn. Although well maintained, the dirt road went on for miles with no sign of civilization. Even the sight of a herd of sheep would have been welcome, just to reassure myself that I wasn't the only creature out there. Perhaps on cue, the June sky began to cloud over. Thus, you can imagine the relief I felt

when I soon arrived at 3 Horse Ranch Vineyards. Like an oasis amongst tumbleweed hills, the vineyard appeared. Martha Cunningham came out to greet me. An attractive, neatly dressed woman, Martha has a decidedly Idaho ranch style and a winning smile. She informed me that her husband, Gary Cunningham, wasn't there, but he would be at the Savor Idaho wine event in Boise that weekend. I finished my visit by taking some photos before the skies unleashed.

At Savor Idaho, I had a chance to meet Gary and sample some 3 Horse Ranch Vineyards wines. The weather was warm, and I pretty much stuck to the refreshing whites, asking for a double sample of a nice, cool viognier with floral notes. If you have a predilection for Rhône varietals, as this WineTrail trekker does, your ship has come in: 3 Horse Ranch offers viognier, roussanne, a viognier/roussanne blend and syrah for your tasting pleasure. Even its rosé has a healthy dose of grenache added. But if southern France varietals don't excite you, this winery's pinot gris, chardonnay, riesling, merlot and Bordeaux blend of cabernet sauvignon and merlot will surely do the trick; they did for me. (See "Decoding an Idaho Wine Label" in Appendix B which highlights their wine label.)

Gary mentioned that noted winemaker Greg Koenig of Koenig Distillery & Winery is a fan of 3 Horse Ranch fruit, using it — among a wide assortment of other vineyards' fruit — to handcraft his premium wines.

Gary also made a point of telling me that the 3 Horse Ranch Vineyards is USDA Certified Organic. When it comes to organic viticulture, no herbicides, insecticides, pesticides or chemical fertilizers are used, and only naturally occurring substances are applied. We're talking sustainable farming practices here, with considerable use of favorable insects, cover crops, mulch and good ol' hand hoeing to attack the weeds.

At 3 Horse Ranch Vineyards, Idaho grapes meet sustainable farming practices, and the result is a romance with the tongue, now and for future generations.

3 HORSE RANCH VINEYARDS
opened: 2003
winemaker(s): Greg Koenig
location: 5900 Pearl Road, Eagle, ID 83616
phone: 208-863-6561
web: www.3horseranchvineyards.com
e-mail: info@3horseranchvineyards.com
picnic area: Yes
fee: Small tasting fee refundable with purchase
hours: Thursday through Sunday 11–6 or
by appointment
lat: 43.834656 **long:** -116.402226

Gary Cunningham

DIRECTIONS: From I-84 take exit 25 and turn right (east) onto ID-44 and proceed about 12.5 miles. Turn left (north) onto SR-44 [W State St.] and go 2.7 miles. Turn left (north) onto SR-16 [Emmett Hwy] and go 6.3 miles. Turn right (east) onto W Chaparral Rd and go 3.1 miles. Bear left onto Pearl Rd and go 2.5 miles to winery.

From Boise, take I-184 [US-20] and travel toward US-26 / Garden City / Fairgrounds. Turn right (north) onto SR-44 [N Glenwood St.] and continue on SR-44 for about 10.5 miles (road name changes). Turn right (north) onto SR-16 [Emmett Hwy] and go 6.3 miles. Turn right (east) onto W Chaparral Rd and go 2.5 miles to 3 Horse Ranch Vineyards.

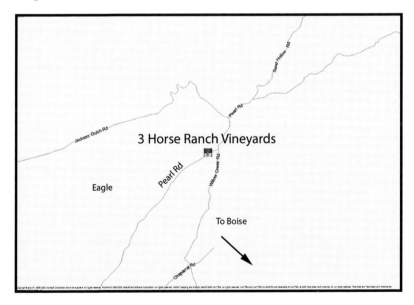

Woodriver Cellars 2

Owner Dave Buich must know a thing or two about having fun. Where else can you go to play bocce while juggling a glass of chardonnay? Some folks see wine as an end in itself, but others view wine as a complement to the good things in life — be it food, music, or bocce. Clearly, the spacious grounds of Woodriver Cellars are all about enjoying life's pleasures — with wine in hand, of course. As the winery itself explains in its bio on Twitter.com, "Woodriver Cellars combines award-winning wine, fun events, live music, stunning art, and beautiful grounds to develop the total sensory experience." Bingo.

All that's true, but it's also clear that the centerpiece of Woodriver Cellars is its wine.

Located in Eagle, Idaho, Woodriver Cellars' renovated 800-square-foot tasting room provides a bistro-like setting for tasting wine (often accompanied by live music). Using grapes from Woodriver Vineyards, located at an elevation of 2,200 feet in the Snake River AVA, Neil Glancey creates premium small-lot wines. It's a manageable assortment to sample and includes delectable riesling, sauvignon blanc, chardonnay, a crisp rosé, Bordeaux reds, and a surprising port-style dessert wine. I say surprising because this delightful drink gave me the urge to retire to the study, don a smoking jacket and light up a cigar.

Once fortified with Woodriver Cellars wine, make a point of walking the spacious grounds to check out the facilities. Included on your tour (depending upon the season) are gardens fragrant with wisteria and roses, four bocce courts, and a 6,000-square-foot tent for hosting weddings, corporate events, or swanky art shows. Time permitting, peek into the generously sized bridal room for prenuptial preparations; those floor-to-ceiling mirrors are always a hit. For the guys, I suspect that the groom's party may find solace in the spacious Barrel Room, where they might have toasted the lucky couple (or gotten toasted) the night before at the rehearsal dinner.

At this point in your visit, you should have some appreciation for Woodriver's slogan, "There's always something happening at Woodriver Cellars." If not, I recommend that you go back to the tasting room and order a glass of its reserve Bordeaux blend. With its rich cherry and black pepper flavors, long finish, and perfectly balanced tannins, it might just inspire you to lob a few bocce balls.

WOODRIVER CELLARS
opened: 2008
winemaker(s): Neil Glancey
location: 3705 Highway 16, Eagle, ID 83616
phone: 208-286-9463
web: www.woodrivercellars.com
e-mail: cfranca@woodrivercellars.com
picnic area: Yes
wheelchair access: Yes
weddings: Yes
fee: Tasting fee may apply
hours: Thursdays and Sundays 11–6; Fridays and
Saturdays 11–10
lat: 43.726027 **long:** -116.461951

DIRECTIONS: From downtown Boise go west on I-184 [US-20] about 1 mile. Bear right onto US-20 [US-26] and go 3.1 miles. Turn right (north) onto SR-44 [N Glenwood St.] and go 1.3 miles. Turn left onto SR-44 [W State St.] and continue 9.4 miles. Turn right (north) onto SR-16 [Emmett Hwy] and arrive at 3705 Hwy 16 in 2.4 miles.

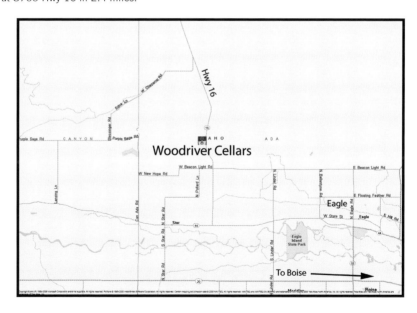

Snake River Winery 3

Located in BoDo (Boise's trendy downtown district), the Snake River Winery tasting room is the perfect place to go before or after dinner or a movie. Situated across the street from the Bonefish Grill and P. F. Chang's China Bistro, this hidden gem of a tasting room is often an unexpected but welcomed discovery by many visitors to this nightlife.

The brainchild of owners Scott and Susan DeSeelhorst, the tasting room features a broad assortment of wine-related gifts and a generous portfolio of complimentary wines to sample. Knowledgeable pouring staff escorts visitors through an international cavalcade of wines, including varietals from France, Germany, Austria, Italy, Spain, and Portugal — truly a United Nations of wines! There's sure to be a wine to please every palate, but

whatever your particular penchant, be sure to sample the Austrian-derived Zweigelt red wine. This hearty grape (actually a hybrid of Blaufränkisch and St. Laurent varietals) does well in frost-prone regions such as Idaho.

Perhaps the real story behind Snake River Winery, however, is the 75-acre Arena Valley Vineyard, owned by Scott and Susan, and located in southwest Idaho's Snake River AVA. The DeSeelhorsts apply organic methods to culture exquisite fruit for themselves and other wineries. They know every acre of this cobblestoned property and, as part of their canopy management program, train every shoot and prune each vine. The result is intensely flavored grapes, and, I am sure, some great summer tans.

Although many winemakers start their careers by earning college degrees in enology and viticulture, Scott's background is in the restaurant business. He's a culinary guy by trade, and thus it's only natural that his interest in pairing food with great wine led him to make wine. As he states on his website, "I treat winemaking like cooking. You start with raw ingredients, combine them in a particular manner, cook or finish the dish, and present the finished product. The key to cooking and winemaking is using the best ingredients, and with wine, of course, that means the grapes."

If you're seeking some food-friendly wine and like a good value (who doesn't?), plan on picking up a bottle (or two) of Snake River Winery's SGM Rhône-style blend of syrah, grenache and mourvedre. At about $18 a bottle, this wonderfully approachable wine is the perfect accompaniment to spicy dishes such as baby back ribs fresh off the barbie. Yummy!

Scott DeSeelhorst

SNAKE RIVER WINERY
opened: 2000
winemaker(s): Scott DeSeelhorst
location: 786 West Broad Street, Boise, ID 83702
phone: 208-345-9463
web: www.snakeriverwinery.com
e-mail: info@snakeriverwinery.com
wheelchair access: Yes
gift shop: Yes
fee: Complimentary wine tasting
hours: Tuesday through Saturday 10:30–7:30, Sunday 12–5; Closed Monday
lat: 43.590418 **long:** -116.311889

DIRECTIONS: From I-84, take exit 49 toward I-184 / City Center and proceed 4.5 miles. Road name changes to Myrtle St. [US-26]. Continue .4 miles. Turn left onto S 8th St. and arrive at W Broad St. where Snake River Winery is located.

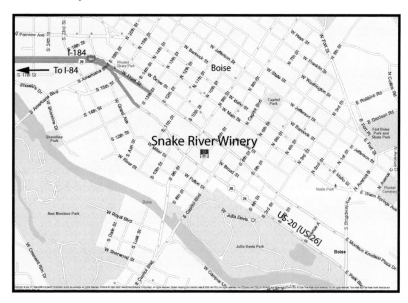

Indian Creek Winery 4

Pulling into Indian Creek Winery off McDermott Road in Kuna, I realized that I was only 20 miles from Boise — but it seemed a world away. The landscaped grounds leading to the Indian Creek Winery seemed like they could easily accommodate a par 3 golf course. A black dog greeted me with wet nose and inquisitive eyes. I later learned that her name is Dahlia; once a shelter dog, she's still a little skittish.

With rows of vineyards at my back, I walked up to the tasting-room door. As soon as I saw the signage on the door noting that "It's Wine Thirty," I knew I was in for a treat.

Bill and Mui Stowe, together with Bill's brother Mike and good friend Rich Ostrogorsky, established Indian Creek Winery in 1987. Since then, the winery has been on a roller coaster ride, with success followed by an occasional winter freeze destroying grapevines and doing a number on the inventory. But despite being subject to the vagaries of Mother Nature, the group has succeeded.

The day-to-day winery functions are in the able hands of daughter Tammy Stowe-McClure and her husband, Mike. Both possess youth, drive, and wisdom beyond their years. During my winery tour, Mike used his thief to extract pinot noir from a French oak barrel and handed me a generous pour. Its light ruby color, soft mouth feel and bright cherry notes struck me as pure pinot noir. I must have given Mike that "What are you doing making pinot noir in sultry southern Idaho?" look. "Believe it or not, it's the wine we are known for," he said.

While Indian Creek Winery enjoys a reputation for its pinot noir, it also produces chardonnay, riesling, cabernet sauvignon, Malbec, syrah, a red blend with the engaging name of Star Garnet, and occasional gewürztraminers and late harvest dessert wine. To satisfy the market's penchant for slightly sweet wine, it also produces a white pinot noir; year after year, this wine has proven to be one of Indian Creek's top sellers.

It turns out that multi-talented Tammy is also a graphic artist, and she designs custom wine labels for weddings, private companies, and special events. At a recent fund-raiser for the Idaho Humane Society, Tammy created a custom label for the highest bidder, which featured the bidder's dog. It's evident that giving back to the community — and to its critters — is second nature for this deeply rooted family.

Mike McClure

INDIAN CREEK WINERY
opened: 1987
winemaker(s): Mike McClure
location: 1000 North McDermott Road,
Kuna, ID 83634
phone: 208-922-4791
web: www.indiancreekwinery.com
e-mail: icwinery@mindspring.com
picnic area: Yes
weddings: Yes
gift shop: Yes
fee: Complimentary wine tasting
hours: Saturday and Sunday 12–5 or by appointment
lat: 43.496927 **long:** -116.473299

DIRECTIONS: From Nampa follow Greenhurst Rd towards Kuna until you reach McDermott Rd and go right (south) for about 3 miles. Winery is on the left.

Alternatively, if coming from Nampa, take 12th Ave. south until it becomes a State Hwy and go left on Deer Flat Rd. Continue until McDermott Rd and then go right. Indian Creek Winery is about .5 miles south.

From Boise take I-84 west about 5 miles to exit 44 towards Kuna / Meridian. Head south toward Kuna on S Meridian Rd into the town of Kuna. Go across railroad tracks and over bridge (Kuna Mora Rd). Continue for 3 miles and take a right on McDermott Rd. Winery is .5 miles on the right.

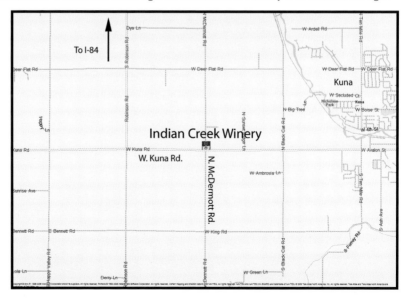

Snake River East

WINE COUNTRY

Thousand Springs
Wine Trail

Thousand Springs Winery

For the 68-mile **Thousand Springs Wine Trail** (and Scenic Byway), pack a camera and budget plenty of time for scenic pit stops. Hagerman Valley, Snake River, Hagerman Fossil Beds National Monument, Thousand Springs, and a number of national and state fish hatcheries and wildlife management areas are just some of the attractions along the **Thousand Springs Wine Trail**. Our swirling begins at Cold Springs Winery, conveniently located off I-84 in Hammett. Take time to walk through its vineyards. Next up is Carmela Vineyards at historic Glenns Ferry; this is where Oregon Trail pioneers made the perilous Snake River crossing. Meandering east, your next stop is Holesinsky Winery in Buhl, where you may meet a young winemaker using the *sur lie* (French for "on the lees") winemaking style. Farther down the road you come to the spectacular 82-acre Snyder Winery, with its commanding view of the valley. From here, an hour-and-a-half drive north on the **Thousand Springs Wine Trail** takes you to Frenchman's Gulch Winery, located in one of America's great destination resorts, Sun Valley. A generous pour of Frenchman's Gulch Ketchum Cuvée goes great with just about anything at any time — after all, it must be 5 p.m. somewhere.

Thousand Springs WineTrail

1 Cold Springs Winery
2 Carmela Vineyards

3 Holesinsky Winery
4 Snyder Winery

5 Frenchman's Gulch Winery

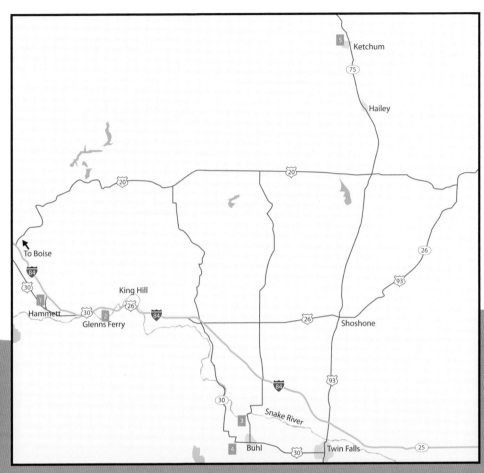

Region:	**Snake River Wine Country East**
# of tasting rooms on tour:	**5**
Estimate # of days for tour:	**2**
Getting around:	**Car**

Tips:
- ❑ Winery eats: Carmela Vineyards and Snyder Winery feature restaurants with excellent fare. Come hungry.
- ❑ Winery stays: Carmela Vineyards provides overnight lodging in comfy cabins. Snyder Winery offers a guest house with all the creature comforts in a gorgeous setting.
- ❑ Ketchum/Sun Valley offers lodging and terrific restaurants galore. For dinner, choices about. Globus Restaurant, Christina's, Ketchum Grill, Sawtooth Club, Ciro Restaurant, Trail Creek Cabin, Roosevelt Tavern and Grille are just some of many choices.

Cold Springs Winery ①

Before meeting him, I had a general idea of who William "Bill" Ringert was. I knew his résumé included stints as a B-25 pilot for the U.S. Air Force, that he attended the University of Idaho obtaining a degree in agriculture, and later earned a law degree from Southern Methodist University and went on to specialize as a water-rights attorney, somehow finding time to be a state senator as well. Impressive indeed, but all that background bio stuff faded when I shook his hand and met his friendly eyes. Bill was busy getting ready to make the hour drive to Boise for a wine-tasting event and only had a few minutes. Still, my brief encounter with Bill was enough to convince me that he focuses on two things in life: devotion to family (especially his wife and winery co-owner, Bing) and passion for Cold Springs Winery.

Taking exit 112 off the I-84 freeway revealed the verdant rows of his 33-acre vineyard. Handmade signs tout the vineyard's varieties of *Vitis vinifera*, including chardonnay, riesling, and syrah. As I approached, the winery dog, Rags, sauntered over to greet me. It was clear she had been enjoying a dip in the nearby reserve pond. While wondering what breed she was, the tasting-room door opened and, with broom in hand, Julia Heath welcomed me.

Every baseball team needs a utility player who can play various positions. For the Cold Springs "team," Julia is that person. Today she was wearing her tasting-room hat, but on other days, she is the vineyard manager; those handmade signs for the vineyard are her creations.

At about that time, Bill arrived in the tasting room and noted that Jamie Martin of Hagerman, Idaho, is his winemaker and it is Jamie who is charged with creating about 4,000 cases annually of chardonnay, viognier, riesling, pinot noir, merlot, cabernet franc, cabernet sauvignon, and syrah. I found all his wines distinctive and enjoyable, but his best seller, Hot Rod Red, a blend of syrah, merlot, and cabernet franc, stopped me in my tasting tracks. As I was imagining this wine paired with a barbecued steak, Bill mentioned that "Jamie likes to do blends." At only $15 a bottle, I sprung for two bottles, and while doing so wondered how I was going to pack these babies in my already crammed suitcase for the flight home. Life has its challenges — they should all be this sweet!

COLD SPRINGS WINERY
opened: 2002
winemaker(s): Jamie Martin
location: 7853 West Ringert Lane,
Hammett, ID 83627
phone: 208-366-7993
web: www.coldspringswinery.com
e-mail: coldspringswines@aol.com
picnic area: Yes
fee: Complimentary wine tasting
hours: Saturday and Sunday 12–5
or appointment only
lat: 42.965694 **long:** -115.545642

Bill Ringert

DIRECTIONS: Cold Springs Winery is located along I-84 approximately 60 miles east of downtown Boise and 65 miles west of Twin Falls. **Take I-84** east to exit 112, turn left onto Hammett Hill Road and take the first right onto West Ringert Lane.

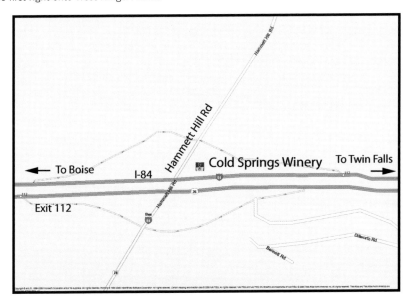

Carmela Vineyards 2

The hour-long drive on I-84 from Boise to Glenns Ferry took me past a wind farm. I noticed as I watched them in the distance that the giant windmills weren't rotating. It later occurred to me that the windmills' stillness and the darkening clouds overhead were early warning signs that Mother Earth soon would be generating her own electricity. The air was still. It was an eerie quiet.

As I pulled onto the grounds of Carmela Vineyards, rows of trees framed the chateau-inspired winery in front of me. I grabbed my camera and hopped out of my rental car. As I snapped away, I noticed that between the winery and the adjacent vineyards were signs directing visitors to the restaurant, bar, RV park, golf course and overnight cabins — the definitive destination winery! **WineTrail Tip**: Situated nearby is Three Island Crossing

State Park, offering easy-to-digest historical information at its Oregon Trail History and Education Center. A must-see.

However, the real kicker for me was discovering that this is the only tasting room in Idaho that has a full liquor license. If you don't have a penchant for wine, you can order a Budweiser. I noticed one guy at the bar nursing Crown Royal Whisky on ice. But I stuck to the wine list and paid the $5 tasting fee (good toward wine purchases) to sample my way selectively through a tasting list, which included riesling, semillon, chardonnay, cabernet franc, merlot, cabernet sauvignon, a Bordeaux blend called Red Meritage and a sweet white wine. Through prior research I had learned that owner Roger Jones features wines showcasing the Snake River appellation, and that Carmela Vineyards produces about 14,000 cases annually. The wines have a wallet-friendly price. At $17.99 a bottle, the Carmela Idaho Merlot had me reaching for my Visa.

About then the skies opened up. A lightning storm ensued, unleashing torrential rain — and I mean a downpour of biblical proportions. I thought about my drive to Carmela and the motionless wind turbines — the calm before the storm, indeed. So much for the photo shoot; I'd just have to return another day. Shrugging my shoulders, I retreated to the restaurant and opted for the buffet line, which featured three-napkin ribs and an amazing dessert bar. I decided to forgo ordering a Crown Royal Whisky and instead opted for my newly purchased bottle of merlot, which turned out to be the perfect accompaniment to the food — and the tempest outside.

CARMELA VINEYARDS
winemaker(s): Roger Jones
location: 795 West Madison, Glenns Ferry, ID 83623
phone: 208-366-2313
web: www.carmelavineyards.com
e-mail: carmelavineyards@rtci.net
picnic area: Yes
weddings: Yes
gift shop: Yes
tours: Yes
fee: Small tasting fee refundable with purchase
hours: Daily 8 a.m. until bar closes
lat: 42.945689 **long:** -115.30621

DIRECTIONS: Carmela Vineyards is located off I-84 halfway between Boise and Twin Falls, on the scenic Snake River within walking distant of Three Island State Park.

Heading east on I-84 about 25 miles past Mountain Home take exit 120 toward Glenns Ferry. Turn right (south) onto I-84 Bus [N Bannock Ave.] and proceed .5 miles. Turn left (east) onto I-84 Bus [W 1st Ave.] and go .4 miles. Turn right (south) onto N Commercial St. and continue .5 miles. Road name changes to W Madison Ave. Go .6 miles and arrive at 795 W Madison Ave.

Heading west on I-84 about 6 miles past Twin Falls take exit 121 and turn left (south) onto I-84 Bus [King Hill Loop]. Keep straight on I-84 Bus [E 1st Ave.] and proceed .7 miles. Turn left (south) onto N Commercial St. and go .5 miles. Road name changes to W Madison Ave. and arrive at winery in .6 miles.

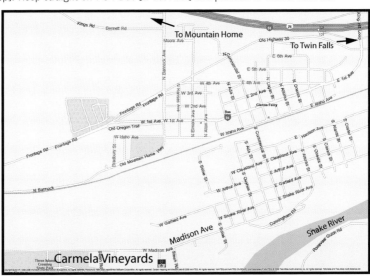

Holesinsky Winery 3

To paraphrase an old saying by Señor Cervantes, "The proof of the wine is in the drinking." And in the case of Buhl, Idaho's Holesinsky Winery, its wines have proven themselves beyond a shadow of a doubt. Owner/winemaker James Holesinsky's creations have continued to rack up awards, including a double gold for his 2008 Rosé at the 2009 Idaho Wine Festival & Competition.

If the competition had been handing out "green" ribbons, he would have won one of those as well. Holesinsky Winery represents a growing number of Idaho wineries going organic. James' 18-acre vineyard in the Snake River appellation is USDA Certified Organic — no small task given the certification's rigorous requirements. Chemical pesticides, herbicides, and insecticides are verboten for at least three years prior to certification. As James states on his Facebook page, "We're organic from soil to bladder." Going beyond growing organic grapes, Holesinsky Winery is striving to achieve

"biodynamic" status in the future. Biodynamic viticulture treats the vineyard and surrounding space as a harmonic ecosystem. This may sound rather woo-woo, but this particular approach, a growing movement worldwide, produces highly acclaimed wines.

Using organically grown grapes is fundamental to making Holesinsky wines, but that's just the start. James is a chemist and a graduate of University of California, Davis' Viticulture and Enology program. Armed with this background and the influence of select Washington winemakers (e.g., Rick Small at Woodward Canyon, Charles Smith at K Vintners, and Mike Moore at Blackwood Canyon) 30-year-old James has developed his own winemaking style. He adheres to Old World French *sur lie* method to age his wine (i.e., barrel aging wine on its lees, or spent yeast), shunning fining (clarification), and filtering his wines to preserve the wine's full flavors.

I had my second pour of Holesinsky Winery's refreshingly spritzy rosé when I eyed a syrah with the curious name "Syrah?" on the label. My interest was diverted, however, when James' parents Barbara and Frank arrived at the tasting room, sporting summer tans and offering warm handshakes. It was clear that the Holesinskys are a close-knit family.

As I drove away, mulling over my visit, it occurred to me that Holesinsky Winery's dedication to sustainability goes beyond using recycled paper for their wine labels; it extends to preserving an Idaho lifestyle, having respect for the land and creating award-winning wines for today and for the future.

HOLESINSKY WINERY
opened: 2001
winemaker(s): James Holesinsky
location: 4477A Valley Steppe Road, Buhl, ID 83316
phone: 208-420-9887
web: www.holesinsky.com
e-mail: james@holesinsky.com
picnic area: Yes
fee: Complimentary wine tasting
hours: Open most days – call ahead
lat: 42.652223 **long:** -114.758014

Winemaker/owner James Holesinsky

DIRECTIONS: From I-84 take exit 141 toward US-26 / US-30 / Gooding / Hagerman. Turn left onto US-30 and proceed about 10 miles. Turn left onto E 4800 N and go .2 miles. Road name changes to River Rd. Continue 6.4 miles (keeping left) and turn right onto N 1500 Rd E [Clear Lakes Rd] and go 1.5 miles. Turn right onto Valley Steppe Dr. and go .6 miles to arrive at 4477 Valley Dr.

From Twin Falls take US-30 [2nd Ave N] 15.3 miles and turn right onto Clear Lakes Ave. Continue 1 mile. Road name changes to N 1500 Rd E [Clear Lakes Rd]. Proceed 2.8 miles and turn left (west) onto Valley Steppe Drive .6 miles and look for signs to the winery.

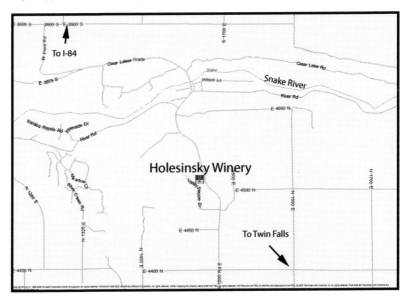

Snyder Winery ④

Evidently, Russ and Claudia Snyder failed to get the memo explaining the concept of "retirement." It's not in their lexicon. While residing in Salt Lake City, where Russ directed sales for a $180 million lumber company, the couple dreamed of owning their own vineyard and winery. Acting on that dream, they bought a dilapidated farm in Buhl in 1999 that required considerable rehabilitation and sweat equity. A consuming passion has a way of conquering such formidable projects.

Now fully retired from corporate life in Salt Lake City, Russ and Claudia can devote all of their time to their 82-acre Shangri-La, with its commanding view of the farming valley. While enjoying a glass of wine on the spacious patio with the owners, I surveyed gazebo-crowned gardens, koi-inhabited ponds, trout farms and hayfields in the distance, the Snyders' herd of cows (the bull's name is Woody), and 4 acres of *Vitis vinifera* grapes. Claudia noted, "Visitors are usually surprised when they come here. There's a lot to see and experience… especially with a glass of wine."

Did I mention that the Snyders offer lodging and fine dining? Yep, they converted a cabin into a charming guesthouse that has all the amenities. Inside their spacious two-story residence, the first floor houses the tasting room and Steak House restaurant, open for dinner Friday and Saturday nights (call for hours). **WineTrail Tip:** Ask for the corner table by the fireplace; the panoramic view perfectly complements the cabernet sauvignon and rib-eye steak.

Snyder Winery (formerly Blue Rock Winery) is a destination winery, and not only for individual WineTrail trekkers. If you need a place to host your next corporate or family event, this is it. For those planning a wedding, Snyder Winery provides generous grounds, a full kitchen, a guesthouse for the bride, and plenty of wine to celebrate the occasion. No doubt the Buhl High School Reunion Committee is eyeing Snyder Winery for its 20-year hoopla.

This winery offers a sanctuary of sorts, where visitors can experience Russ and Claudia's dream of "wine and roses." Make a point of chatting with the Snyders and ask them their secret for achieving such Herculean goals. (Their daily to-do list must be several pages long.) I suspect triple lattes provide a kick-start each morning, with glasses of Snyder Chardonnay in the evening to end the day on a smooth note.

SNYDER WINERY
winemaker(s): Russ and Claudia Snyder
location: 4060 North 1200 East, Buhl, ID 83316
phone: 208-543-6938
web: www.snyderwinery.com
picnic area: Yes
weddings: Yes
fee: Tasting fee may apply
hours: April through December Friday through Sunday, 12 to dusk. Otherwise by appointment
lat: 42.588129 **long:** -114.809762

DIRECTIONS: **Heading east on I-84** take exit 141 turn right (west) onto I-84 Bus [US-26]. Turn left (south) onto US-30 and continue about 12 miles. Turn right (south) onto N 1200 E and go 1 mile. Turn left (east) onto E 4100 Rd N [E Deep Creek Rd], then immediately turn right (south) onto N 1200 E and go .5 miles and arrive at Snyder Winery.

From Twin Falls go northwest onto US-30 (2nd Ave. N). Continue for about 16 miles. Turn left on Main Street. Turn left on Burley Ave. W. Road name changes to E 4100 Road N. Turn left (south) onto N 1200 E, arriving at 4060 N 1200 E.

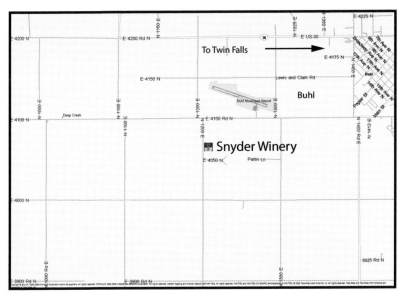

Frenchman's Gulch Winery 🄯

"Altitude fermentation," Stephen "Mac" McCarthy responded to my query about how he gets his wines to taste so bloody good. Mac was making the case that Ketchum's elevation of 5,750 feet contributes to prolonged fermentation process. The result is velvety smooth reds with complex layers and lasting finishes. Mac went on to explain that the high altitude requires an extra-long period of fermentation before pressing and barrel aging. This, he feels, translates into premium wines and reinforces his decision, made many years ago, to move from Chicago to this high-altitude Idaho ski resort.

I was swirling and sniffing Frenchman's Gulch Winery's cabernet sauvignon when Mac's dog, Bo, made a guest appearance. Sporting a "bohawk" summer 'do, Bo circled and planted himself at my feet. I asked Mac about his source of grapes; after all, Sun Valley is a long way from vineyards. He explained that he acquires his grapes from some of the finest

vineyards in Eastern Washington's Columbia Valley. His relationship with Washington grape growers spans many "leaf years." During harvest, Mac and his team make 10 roundtrip runs to Washington to fetch his grapes.

From these grapes, Mac handcrafts about 1,300 cases of premium wines a year, including chardonnay, merlot, cabernet sauvignon, syrah, and a Bordeaux blend named Ketchum Cuvée. These are small-lot wines involving family and friends crushing and pressing the grapes. Feet get purple, smiles abound, and the harvest is celebrated with lots of wine. Of course it doesn't hurt that the setting itself is first class: The stone-faced winery and tasting room buildings have a distinct Euro feel, and the surrounding mountains add to the sense of place. Given this setting, I suspect Mac has to turn away volunteers.

While tasting his luscious syrah, I asked Mac where he hopes to take Frenchman's Gulch Winery. He responded that he just wants to make good wine and sell it at an affordable price. He'd like to keep production to about 1,300 cases annually, and with that production, show the world that exquisite wines can be made in high-altitude ski country. At this point in our conversation, I began to catch a buzz and thought I'd better switch from swallowing to spitting the wine. Then it dawned on me that my dizziness was brought on by the mile-high altitude, not overindulgence. Heck, what's a little light-headedness — I kept swigging.

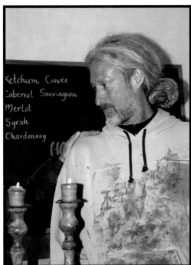

Mac McCarthy

FRENCHMAN'S GULCH WINERY
opened: 2000
winemaker(s): Mac McCarthy
location: 360 9th Street East, Suites 9 and 10, Ketchum, ID 83340
phone: 208-726-0118
web: www.frenchmansgulch.com
e-mail: frenchmansgulch@gmail.com
wheelchair access: Yes
fee: Complimentary wine tasting
hours: Wednesdays and Saturdays, 3–6
lat: 43.684152 **long:** -114.36806

DIRECTIONS: Heading northwest on SR-75 arrive at Ketchum and keep straight onto Warm Spring Rd. Proceed .2 miles and turn right onto 9th St. E and proceed a short distance to the winery at 360 9th St. E.

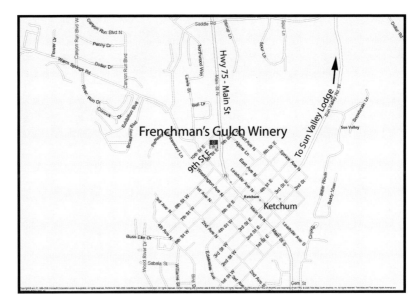

Enjoying the quiet life in Sun Valley

Summer flowers in Ketchum

Cold Springs Winery, Hammett

Bitner Vineyards, Caldwell

Waiting to be discovered

Snyder Winery cattle, Woody second from left

Frenchman's Gulch Winery

Just ripe

Hells Canyon Winery, Caldwell

Carmela Vineyards

Idaho — Great wineries and spectacular colors

By Appointment
WINE COUNTRY

By-Appointment-Only Wineries   78

By-Appointment-Only Wineries
WineTrail

Miceli Vineyards & Winery along the banks of the Snake River

Throughout the Gem State, a number of wineries welcome only visitors who have made an appointment. For experienced WineTrail trekkers, these wineries are often a joy to visit. Why? Because you will have a slice of time to spend alone with the winemaker. There's time to ask questions about their winemaking style, how they got their start and where they hope to take their venture. Often you'll go beyond the tasting room to sample wine right of the barrel or tramp through the vineyard and get a free lesson in horticulture.

Be aware that there is a reason many wineries are open by appointment only. Perhaps the owner/winemaker has a full-time day job that consumes much of their time, or their case production is very limited and inventory is scarce. I know of one Idaho winemaker whose home is a two-hour drive from his winery. Most of the time, that winery's door is locked, and when he's there, his focus is on handcrafting fine wine. Thus, a word to the wise: Call well in advance. Occasionally you can luck out with the "I'm just outside your gates and wondering if you are open" call, but in most cases, these winemakers will need advance warning. By doing so, you are sure to be rewarded with a memorable experience. Cheers!

By-Appointment-Only Wineries

1. TimberRock Winery
2. St. Regulus Unique Wines
3. Parma Ridge Vineyards
4. Miceli Vineyards & Winery
5. Weston Winery & Vineyards
6. Silver Trail Winery
7. Cinder Winery
8. Syringa Winery
9. Vale Wine Co.
10. Fraser Vineyard
11. Thousand Springs Winery
12. Hegy's South Hills Winery

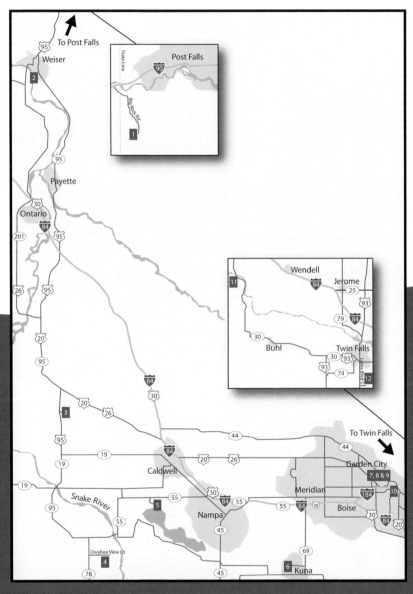

Region:	**Snake River Wine Country East**
# of tasting rooms on tour:	**12**
Estimate # of days for tour:	**Multiple**
Getting around:	**Car**
Key Events:	❏ **Savor Idaho, June, Boise**
	❏ **Sun Valley Wine Auction, July**

TimberRock Winery

When he's not busy with his veterinary practice, winemaker/owner Dr. Kevin Rogers handcrafts small lots of delicious wines. Located in a pristine Post Falls mountain location, TimberRock Winery relies on eastern Washington fruit, producing a wide variety of red and white wines. Open by appointment only when they are available, call well in advance of your desired visit date. **WineTrail Tip:** Be sure and taste his cabernet sauvignon — lovely.

TIMBERROCK WINERY
winemaker(s): Kevin Rogers
location: 2338 South Big Rock Road, Post Falls, ID 83854
phone: 208-777-9669
web: www.timberrockwine.com
e-mail: info@timberrockwine.com
fee: NA
hours: By appointment only
lat: 47.656201 **long:** -117.01773

DIRECTIONS: On I-90 heading east or west, take exit 299 on the Washington side. Go south onto N Spokane Bridge Rd for .2 miles. Road name changes to N Idaho Rd. Continue for .3 miles and keep left onto W Riverview Dr. for .6 miles. Enter Idaho. Turn right onto S Millsap Loop and proceed 1.9 miles. Turn right at S Big Rock Rd and go .7 miles. Arrive at 2338 S Big Rock Rd at the winery.

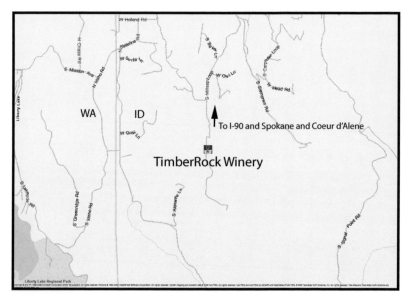

www.winetrailsnw.com/wineries/timberrock_winery

St. Regulus Unique Wines

2

Winemaker Dave Rule developed his own fermenting equipment to produce small batches of reds, whites, and rosés — hence the "Unique" in the winery's moniker. An image of the 11th-century St. Regulus tower in Scotland adorns these wine labels. The winery is located in Weiser in southwest Idaho, which is also where Dave and his wife, Judy, reside.

Judy Rule

ST. REGULUS UNIQUE WINES
opened: 2008
winemaker(s): Dave Rule
location: 407 River Dock Road, Weiser, ID 83672
phone: 208-549-8040
web: www.stregulus.com
e-mail: wines@stregulus.com
fee: NA
hours: By appointment only
lat: 44.210724 **long:** -116.952687

DIRECTIONS: From Weiser take Hwy 95 south and go right at River Dock Rd. Continue 2.3 miles to St. Regulus Wines on the right.

From Payette take Hwy 95 north 9.8 miles from last light in Payette. Go left at Airport Rd and proceed 1 mile. Bear right at River Dock Rd. St. Regulus Wines is on the left.

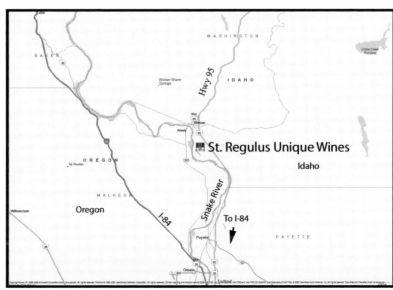

Parma Ridge Vineyards

By-Appointment-Only Wineries

Situated with a view of the Boise River below, Parma Ridge Winery is the creation of winemaker Dick Dickstein. Dick and his wife, Shirley, produce estate wines from the 9.5-acre vineyard located on the property. Dick's delightful wines are matched only by his own charm.

Dick Dickstein

PARMA RIDGE VINEYARDS
opened: 2000
winemaker(s): Dick Dickstein
location: 24509 Rudd Road, Parma, ID 83660
phone: 208-722-6885
web: www.parmaridge.com
e-mail: parmaridge@earthlink.net
fee: NA
hours: By appointment only
lat: 43.726918 **long:** -116.90681

DIRECTIONS: Take I-84 to exit 27. Proceed onto Hwy 19 to Wilder, 3 miles north. Turn right on Bluff Lane, and right again on Rudd Road to top of hill.

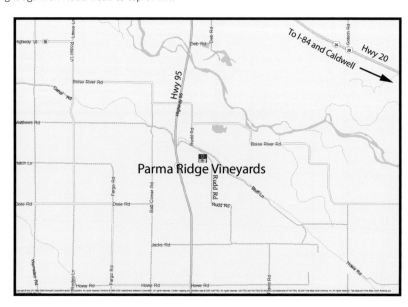

82 **WineTrails**NW www.winetrailsnw.com/wineries/parma_ridge_vineyards

Miceli Vineyards & Winery 4

By-Appointment-Only Wineries

Marvelous Miceli Vineyards & Winery is set beside the Snake River in southwestern Idaho. The brainchild of Jim and Michele Mitchell (who also invested a lot of sweat equity), the winery reflects Jim's Italian roots and, in particular, pays homage to his grandfather Francesco Miceli, who taught Jim the art of winemaking.

MICELI VINEYARDS & WINERY
winemaker(s): Jim Mitchell
location: 8114 Owyhee View Lane, Givens Hot Springs, ID 83641
phone: 208-896-5803
web: www.micelivineyards.com
e-mail: mitchell@speedyquick.net
fee: NA
hours: By appointment only
lat: 43.416225 **long:** -116.706227

DIRECTIONS: From I-84, take exit 33A toward Marsing (south). Road name becomes SR-55 [Karcher Rd]. Travel through the town of Marsing after crossing the Snake River. At SR-78 (Snake River Mart is on the corner), turn left (south) and travel past mile marker 7. The third dirt road to the left (east) is Owyhee View Lane. After turning, bear left at the first and follow the lane to the end. There will be vineyards on your right. The winery is the large white structure on your right.

Coming from Nampa, take SR-45 (12th Ave. Rd South), travel south to SR-78, crossing the Snake River at Walter's Ferry. Turn right (north) on Hwy 78. About 3 miles after passing Givens Hot Springs, Owyhee View Lane is on the right after mile marker 8. Take this lane toward the river, bearing left at the fork. Follow it to the end, passing the vineyards on the right. The winery is the white structure on your right.

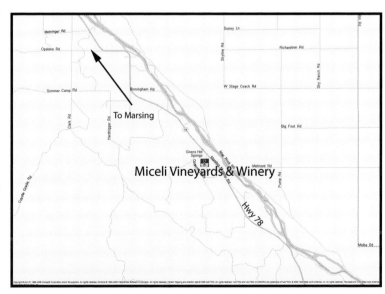

Weston Winery & Vineyards 5 By-Appointment-Only Wineries

Located in Caldwell, Weston Winery is the creation of Cheyne and Murrie Weston. Winemaker Cheyne handcrafts small lots of wine relished by local and visiting fans of fine wine. The friendly, unpretentious winery is located near a number of wineries in the Sunnyslope WineTrail, making this a convenient stop during your visit to the area.

Cheyne and Murrie Weston

WESTON WINERY & VINEYARDS
opened: 1981
winemaker(s): Cheyne Weston
location: 16316 Orchard Street, Caldwell, ID 83605
phone: 208-459-2631
web: None
tours: Yes
fee: NA
hours: By appointment only
lat: 43.596211 **long:** -116.718818

DIRECTIONS: From Caldwell, take I-84 Bus [Blaine St.] .3 miles and bear left (west) onto SR-19 [E Simplot Blvd.] and go .9 miles. Turn left (south) onto Farmway Rd and go 5.2 miles. Turn right (west) and arrive at winery's 16316 Orchard Ave. address.

From Boise, take I-84 west about 14 miles to exit 35. Turn right (north) onto Northside Blvd. and go .2 miles. Turn left (west) onto W Karcher Rd and go 1.5 miles. Road name changes to SR-55 [W Karcher Rd]. Continue 6 miles. Turn left (south) onto Riverside Rd and go .5 miles before turning left (east) onto Orchard Ave. Arrive at 16316 Orchard Ave. in .2 miles.

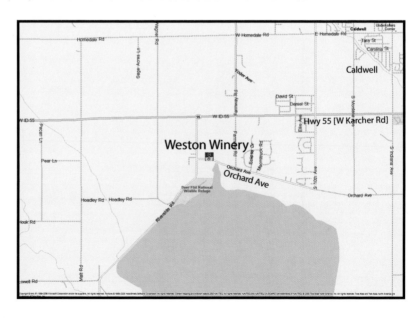

www.winetrailsnw.com/wineries/weston_winery_and_vineyards

Silver Trail Winery 6

Kuna-based Silver Trail Winery features premium wines and ports. Winemaker Nick Nicholas uses locally grown zinfandel to make a tawny port that is aged at least five years in oak. If you enjoy a nice glass (or two) of fine port, be sure to schedule a visit to Silver Trail Winery.

SILVER TRAIL WINERY
winemaker(s): Nick Nicholas
location: 1299 North School Street, Kuna, ID 83634
phone: 208-922-9558
web: www.silvertrailwinery.com
e-mail: info@silvertrailwinery.com
fee: NA
hours: By appointment only
lat: 43.500045 **long:** -116.423574

DIRECTIONS: If traveling east or west on I-84 take exit 44 toward Meridian / Kuna. Go south on SR-69 [S Meridian Rd] for 6.3 miles. Turn right (west) onto E Deer Flat Rd and proceed 1.5 miles. Turn left (south) onto N School St. and travel .2 miles to arrive at Silver Trail Winery.

Cinder Winery 7

One of Idaho's top winemakers, Melanie Krause produces small lots of wine at the Urban Wine-makers Cooperative, located in Garden City, near Boise. Melanie's winemaking résumé includes stints at Chateau Ste. Michelle's Canoe Ridge Estate Winery and Northstar Winery, both in Washington state. Melanie chose the name "Cinder" for the layers of volcanic soil found under Idaho vineyards. From the for-what-it's-worth column, Cinder wines are among the best in Idaho in my opinion!

Melanie Krause

CINDER WINERY
winemaker(s): Melanie Krause
location: 107 East 44th Street, Urban Winemakers Cooperative, Garden City, ID 83714
phone: 208-433-9813
web: www.cinderwines.com
e-mail: joe@cinderwines.com
fee: NA
hours: By appointment only
lat: 43.633789 **long:** -116.254354

DIRECTIONS: Located at the Urban Winemakers Cooperative in Garden City near neighboring Boise. **From downtown Boise** take I-184. Bear right onto US-20 [US-26] and go about 1.5 miles. Turn right onto E 44th St. and arrive at Urban Winemakers Cooperative in the old Quality Produce building.

www.winetrailsnw.com/wineries/cinder_winery

Syringa Winery 8

Winemaker/owner Mike Crowley specializes in making wines using grapes from the Snake River Valley appellation. Idaho's state flower — the syringa — graces the labels of his wine bottles. Syringa Winery is located at the Urban Winemakers Cooperative, sharing space and equipment with Cinder Winery and Vale Wine Co. Be sure to sample Syringa's Primitivo (zinfandel) wine. Delizioso!

Mike Crowley

SYRINGA WINERY
opened: 2007
winemaker(s): Mike Crowley
location: 107 East 44th Street, Urban Winemakers Cooperative, Garden City, ID 83714
phone: 208-376-4023
web: www.syringawinery.com
e-mail: mcrowley@syringawinery.com
fee: NA
hours: By appointment only
lat: 43.633789 **long:** -116.254354

DIRECTIONS: Located at the Urban Winemakers Cooperative in Garden City near neighboring Boise. **From downtown Boise** take I-184. Bear right onto US-20 [US-26] and go about 1.5 miles. Turn right onto E 44th St. and arrive at Urban Winemakers Cooperative in the old Quality Produce building.

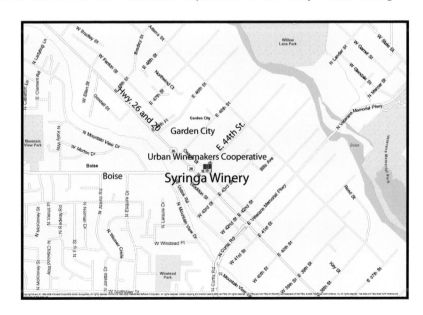

Vale Wine Co.

John Danielson and a group of partners launched Vale Wine Co. with the goal of using estate-grown grapes to produce wine. John and his wife, Vicki, manage the day-to-day operations of producing and distributing their wine. Vale Wine Co is located at the Urban Winemakers Cooperative, sharing space and equipment with Cinder Winery and Syringa Winery. Vale Wine Co. wines can also be sampled at Coyotes in Caldwell.

John Danielson

VALE WINE CO.
opened: 2008
winemaker(s): John Danielson
location: 107 East 44th Street,
Urban Winemakers Cooperative,
Garden City, ID 83714
phone: 208-409-8950
web: www.valewineco.com
e-mail: john@valewineco.com
fee: NA
hours: By appointment only
lat: 43.633789 **long:** -116.254354

DIRECTIONS: Located at the Urban Winemakers Cooperative in Garden City near neighboring Boise. **From downtown Boise** take I-184. Bear right onto US-20 [US-26] and go about 1.5 miles. Turn right onto E 44th St. and arrive at Urban Winemakers Cooperative in the old Quality Produce building.

Fraser Vineyard

By-Appointment-Only Wineries

Fraser Vineyard wines are the creation of winemaker/owner Bill Fraser, whose winery is located in Boise. Bill's wines consistently win accolades from wine lovers (including this writer). A Scottish tartan of the Fraser clan festoons the Fraser Vineyard wine labels. His wines are a great value and would explain why descriptions of his wine are often accompanied by two words: sold out.

FRASER VINEYARD
opened: 2005
winemaker(s): Bill Fraser
location: 1004 La Pointe Street, Boise, ID 83706
phone: 208-345-9607
web: www.fraservineyard.com
e-mail: fraser@fraservineyard.com
fee: NA
hours: By appointment only
lat: 43.608397 **long:** -116.212714

Bill Fraser

DIRECTIONS: From downtown Boise, turn south onto S 9th St. and turn right at Royal Blvd. Turn left at S La Pointe St. and arrive at Fraser Vineyard winery at 1004 La Pointe Street.

From I-84 take Boise Airport/Vista exit and go north on Vista Ave. 2.3 miles. Turn left at S Capitol Blvd and proceed .3 miles. Turn left at W Ann Morrison Park Dr. followed by a quick right at S Lusk St. Go left at W Sherwood St. followed by another right at S La Pointe St. and arrive at the winery.

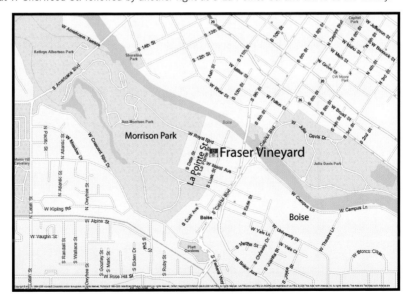

Thousand Springs Winery

11 By-Appointment-Only Wineries

Located in Hagerman, in south-central Idaho, Thousand Springs Winery is owned and operated by Paul Monahan and Susan Parslow. In this bucolic setting, WineTrail trekkers experience estate wines from Paul and Susan's 10-acre vineyard, take in wonderful views, and generally have a hard time extricating themselves from such tasty splendor.

Paul Monahan

THOUSAND SPRINGS WINERY
winemaker(s): Paul Monahan
location: 18972 Highway 30, Hagerman, ID 83332
phone: 208-837-4001
web: www.thousandspringswinery.com
e-mail: paulandsusan@thousandspringswinery.com
fee: NA
hours: By appointment only
lat: 42.77553 **long:** -114.888395

DIRECTIONS: Heading east on I-84 from Boise, take exit 141 toward US-26 / US-30 / Gooding / Hagerman and turn right (west) onto I-84 Bus [US-26] for .2 miles. Turn left (south) onto US-30 and go 10 miles and arrive at Thousand Springs Winery.

Heading west on I-84 from Twin Falls, take exit 155 and go left (west) onto SR-46 Spur [2950 S]. Road name changes to Hagerman Hwy. Proceed about 5 miles. Road name changes to 2900 S and then to Vader Grade. Continue 3.7 miles and turn left (south) onto US-30 [1000 E] and go .8 miles and arrive at winery.

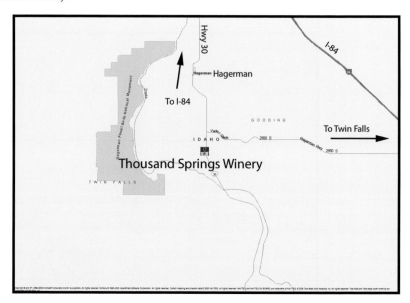

Hegy's South Hills Winery By-Appointment-Only Wineries

Located four miles south of Twin Falls, Frank and Crystal Hegy's winery is one of Idaho's smallest. Typical vintages include chardonnay, chenin blanc, riesling, lemberger, and pinot noir.

HEGY'S SOUTH HILLS WINERY
opened: 1989
winemaker(s): Frank and Crystal Hegy
location: 3099 East 3400 North, Twin Falls, ID 83301
phone: 208-734-6369
web: None
fee: NA
hours: By appointment only
lat: 42.490697 **long:** -114.441001

DIRECTIONS: From Twin Falls take US-30 [2nd Ave. S] .7 miles. Turn right (south) onto Blue Lakes Blvd. S and proceed 4 miles. Turn left (east) onto E 3400 N and go 1 mile and arrive at 3099 E 3400 N.

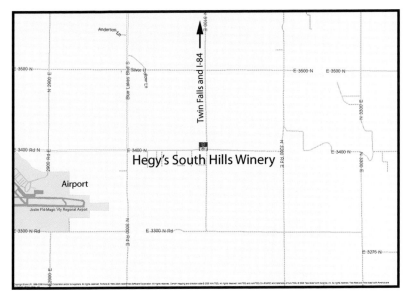

Frenchman's Gulch Winery

Appendix A - Tasting Tips
Wine Tasting 101

The key to tasting wine is to slow down and concentrate.

Beyond that, you just need to swirl, smell and taste. A visual check of the wine simply informs your brain what you are about to taste. Red wine ranges in color from purple, ruby red, deep red, red brown, mahogany, to brown. White wine hues range from yellow green, straw, gold, yellow-brown, amber brown, to brown. It's a good idea to hold your glass up to a white background (a wall or a napkin) to judge the color of the wine. Where the wine is on the color palette informs your brain and gives your taste buds a heads up for what they are about to experience.

Once the wine is poured, some folks like to tilt the glass and observe how the wine flows down the inside of the glass. However, there is no correlation between the "legs" or "tears" on the inside of the glass and the taste itself.

Swirling
A wine just poured needs to stretch its legs and aerate. Swirling lets the wine open up and release aromas. Up to this point, oxygen has been a bad thing; now, oxygen is the wine's best friend. It allows the wine to open up and create a bouquet. Most tasting rooms provide wine glasses roomy enough to swirl the wine without spillage. You need that space between

Indian Creek Winery

the wine and your nose to smell the aroma. If you chance upon a winery that uses little plastic cups or tiny "orange juice glasses," you might consider shortening your visit and moving on to the next winery.

Smelling
The aroma given off by a wine is its "nose." Right after a vigorous swirl, quickly smell the wine by sticking your nose into the glass. Get it as far down as possible. Concentrate and let your imagination run wild as you attempt to describe what you smell. In time, descriptions such as sweaty saddle, cat pee (no kidding), tar, kerosene, burnt match, and asparagus may enter your smelling lexicon. Researchers say that flavor is 75 percent smell and 25 percent taste.

Thirsty glasses ready to be filled at the Koenig Distillery & Winery

No wonder food tastes bland when you have a cold. You can't smell it. Merlot, pinot noir and cabernet sauvignon, have a distinctive smells.

Tasting

Most of us grew up with the understanding that the tongue has certain regions that taste salt, bitter, sweet, and sour. Have you ever seen those drawings of the tongue that depict which part of the tongue tastes what? But according to current research, all taste buds can taste salt, bitter, sweet and sour to varying degrees. Taste buds are on the front of the tongue and the back. That's why you see sommeliers and wine connoisseurs vigorously swishing the wine around their mouth; they are getting the maximum exposure throughout their mouth to taste the wine. While swishing, your brain is also registering other sensations, such as heaviness, roundness, finish, and astringency from the tannins found in the wine. Concentrate for a few seconds while the wine is in your mouth. Swirl it around your mouth and attempt to suck a little air in — without committing a gagging faux pas – to pick up the wine's full flavors.

Remember, slow down and concentrate.

Tasting Room Etiquette

There are definite rules of the road when it comes to visiting tasting rooms, and most involve common sense. Moderation is a good thing. Those little ounces add up. So have a strategy ahead of time and try to stick to it. Here's some WineTrail do's and don'ts:

Do's:

- Drink responsibly — designate a driver or hire a limo.
- Spit or dump as much as you want — that's what those buckets are for!
- Have patience with the wine pourer — don't poodle your way forward with outstretched hand begging for another fill; they'll get to you.
- Have a tasting strategy — choose which wines you would like to sample. If you are only interested in the reds, let your pourer know.

Snake River Winery's tasting room

- Ask questions — tasting room staff are passionate about their wines and anxious to tell you why.
- Purchase wine if you want to — assuming it is in your budget and you like it, spring for it.
- Be open to wines that you believe you will not like — reds, whites, port wines. You might be surprised to learn how delicious chardonnay from Idaho's Snake River Valley can be or how blackberry wine might be a perfect accompaniment to the pound cake you plan to serve.
- Let them know if you like their wine — there's a reason that the pourer is staring at you with an expectant look in their eyes. If you like it, tell them. Winemakers live for such moments.

Don'ts:

- Ask for a second helping — unless you are contemplating purchasing a bottle, or you need a second helping to clarify what you just tasted.
- Feel that you have to purchase a bottle of wine — the winery's primary goal is to provide you a positive experience so you tell your friends and family about it.
- Wear perfumes or colognes — your nose needs to smell the wine.
- Attempt to engage the tasting room staff in esoteric debates — save the Hungarian versus American oak debate for a conversation with the winemaker, not the poor pourer.
- Take anything — the wine glasses are theirs, not yours (unless the tasting fee includes a glass).
- Drink excessively — keep your wits; spit often and pace yourself.

Decoding an Idaho Wine Label

Front

1 **Winery name**

2 **Vintage:** At least 95 percent of the grapes used were harvested in the year shown on the label.

3 **Varietal:** 75 percent of the volume must be composed of the grape varietal named on the label.

4 **Estate grown:** Denotes that the grapes were grown by the winery.

5 **Appellation:** 85 percent of the grapes in this wine must come from the named appellation (e.g., Snake River Valley).

6 **Alcohol content:** Percent alcohol by volume.

Additional Terms:
Reserve wine is a term given to a specific wine to imply that it is of a higher quality than usual, or a wine that has been aged before being sold, or both. Traditionally winemakers would "reserve" some of their best wine rather than sell it immediately, thus the term.

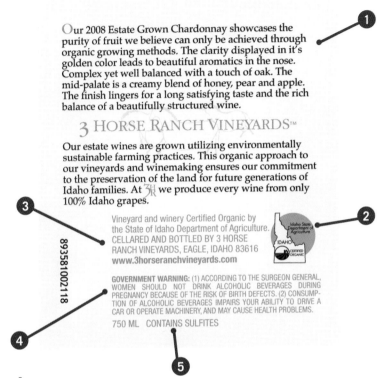

Our 2008 Estate Grown Chardonnay showcases the
purity of fruit we believe can only be achieved through
organic growing methods. The clarity displayed in it's
golden color leads to beautiful aromatics in the nose.
Complex yet well balanced with a touch of oak. The
mid-palate is a creamy blend of honey, pear and apple.
The finish lingers for a long satisfying taste and the rich
balance of a beautifully structured wine.

3 HORSE RANCH VINEYARDS™

Our estate wines are grown utilizing environmentally
sustainable farming practices. This organic approach to
our vineyards and winemaking ensures our commitment
to the preservation of the land for future generations of
Idaho families. At ꓱ we produce every wine from only
100% Idaho grapes.

Vineyard and winery Certified Organic by
the State of Idaho Department of Agriculture.
CELLARED AND BOTTLED BY 3 HORSE
RANCH VINEYARDS, EAGLE, IDAHO 83616
www.3horseranchvineyards.com

GOVERNMENT WARNING: (1) ACCORDING TO THE SURGEON GENERAL,
WOMEN SHOULD NOT DRINK ALCOHOLIC BEVERAGES DURING
PREGNANCY BECAUSE OF THE RISK OF BIRTH DEFECTS. (2) CONSUMP-
TION OF ALCOHOLIC BEVERAGES IMPAIRS YOUR ABILITY TO DRIVE A
CAR OR OPERATE MACHINERY, AND MAY CAUSE HEALTH PROBLEMS.

750 ML CONTAINS SULFITES

Back

① **Descriptive information:** Added information to give consumers more information about the winemaking process for marketing purposes.

② **Growing green designations:** Many Idaho wineries embrace sustainable growing and winemaking practices including organic and biodynamic farm practices. Wineries self-report select designations including a "certified organic" label from the State of Idaho Department of Agriculture.

③ **Produced and bottled by:** Denotes who actually made and bottled the wine and their location. Includes address and contact information (e.g., web site address).

④ **Government warning:** Notice to pregnant women that wine may cause health problems and the ability to drive a car or operate machinery may be impaired by drinking alcohol.

⑤ **Content:** Presence of sulfites and volume (e.g., 750 ml).

Boise River

Idaho Varietals Chart of Whites

Ch_{ardonnay}

Burgundy origins, vigorous and adaptable to many soils. Cool climate grape. Typically aged in oak but trend toward un-oaked. Fruity with terms such as apple, peach, citrus and pineapple used to describe. Very food friendly.

Ge_{würztraminer}

German-Alsatian grape variety reddish-brown thick skinned grape with typical spicy flavor. One of the earliest to mature. Prefers cool climate. Spicy, floral, fruity, lychee, honey and jasmine tea are terms often used to describe. Dry to sweet.

Snake River Valley AVA Profile

Location: Southwest Idaho includes former Lake Idaho bed from Twin Falls in the east to parts of Baker and Malheur counties in eastern Oregon

Size: 8,263 square miles; 5.27 million acres

Weather: 10 to 12 inches of precipitation per year; 142 days average growing season

Soil: Varies but sand, mud silts, loess, and volcanic ash dominate

Topography: Snake River Valley basin surrounded by several mountain ranges; most vineyards between 1,500 and 2,500 feet (high desert).

Mu_{scat}

World's oldest known grape variety. Classic rich nose of dried fruits, raisins, oranges and intense ripe fruit characteristics. Pronounced sweet floral aroma.

Pi_{not gris}

Grayish-hue fruit (gris is French for gray) is called pinot grigio in Italy. Originating in Burgundy, the wine is very terroir dependent ranging in style from crisp, light and dry (Italy) to rich, fat, and honeyed (France's Alsace region and Western U.S.).

Riesling

German white grape originating in the Rhine River Valley. Very terroir expressive, rieslings balance on a fine line between acidity an delicacy. Flavor descriptors include peach, apple, quince and citrus. Riesling pairs wonderfully with grilled fish, chicken, Thai food and summer salads.

Roussanne

Derived from the northern portion of France's Rhône region, often used for blending. The berries are russet colored when ripe — roux is French for the reddish brown color russet, the root for the variety's name. Full-bodied, with flavors of honey and pear.

Sauvignon Blanc

Green skinned grape originating in Bordeaux where it is often blended with semillon. Vigorous with tender skin, produces crisp, dry and refreshing wines. Fruity to grassy depending upon origin and viticulture methods.

Sémillon

Bordeaux derived grape vinified as a single variety or blended – often with sauvignon blanc. Vigorous, found world-wide. By itself, sémillon produces wines that are not well-rounded and very light in color. Blended with sauvignon blanc, the resulting wines can be extraordinary.

Viognier

Golden colored wine with significant cultivation in the northern Rhône region of France. Often blended with other white grapes and syrah. Very fruity bouquet with pronounced floral notes.

Idaho Varietals Chart of Reds

Ba_{rbera}

Italy's third most popular grape grown principally in the Piedmont area, vary significantly from medium body wines to powerful intense wines capable of cellaring. Deep ruby color, pink rim, noticeable levels of tannins and pronounced acidity.

Ca_{bernet Franc}

Black-skinned Bordeaux grape often blended with cabernet sauvignon and merlot. Increasingly, it is vinified by itself. It prefers cooler climate relative to cabernet sauvignon. Aromas include raspberries, cassis, tobacco and floral.

Ca_{bernet}
Sauvignon

Blue-black berries with Bordeaux origins, cabernet sauvignon is the most important grape in the world. Vigorous, the grape prefers warm weather climates. Full-bodied, rich and tannic, it is often blended with merlot and cabernet franc to soften it.

Gr_{enache}

Grenache grape does well in hot, dry regions and strong stalk makes it well suited for windy conditions. Grenache wines are sweet, fruity, and very low in tannins. Often exhibits high alcohol levels (15 to 16%). Widely planted in southern France with origins in Spain.

Le_{mberger}

Called Blaufränkisch in Germany, Lemberger has nuances of merlot and cabernet but with a hard to define spicy note. Mildly tannic with moderate alcohol. Characterized as fruity, light, and lively.

Ma_{lbec}

Ink-dark with robust tannins, malbec is a Bordeaux grape. It's put Argentina on the wine world map. Often blended with other Bordeaux grapes to produce clarets. Characterized by dark fruit notes and herbal aromas.

Me_{rlot}

Popular Bordeaux grape often blended with cabernet sauvignon. Merlot is medium body ("fleshy") noble grape with hints of berry, plum and currant. Consistently described as smooth, it is lighter in color, acid and tannins than cabernet sauvignon.

Mo_{urvèdre}

From southern France's Rhône region, mourvèdre grapes produce garnet-colored wines with spicy, peppery characteristics. Due to high tannins and alcohol levels, it is often blended with Grenache. The grapes are thick-skinned exhibiting blue-black colors.

Pe_{tit Verdot}

A high quality Bordeaux grape used primarily as a blending "seasoning" wine. Full-bodied, deep-colored with peppery, spicy flavor characteristics. High in tannins and alcohol. Increasing popularity as a standalone variety wine in new world.

Pi_{not Noir}

Described as the most finicky of grapes, this Burgundy grape is small, blue-black and thin-skinned in pinecone shaped clusters. Light ruby red, the flavors are often characterized as fresh strawberry to berry jam, spicy, black pepper and cherry.

Sy_{rah}

Vigorous and performs well in different soil types. Rhône derived variety, syrah is big-bodied and capable of aging for many years. Often blended with grenache and mouvrèdre in Rhône. In Australia, syrah is called shiraz.

Te_{mpranillo}

Spain's noble grape, tempranillo is a full-bodied wine ruby red in color. Aromas of berries, plum, tobacco, vanilla, leather and herb describe this wine. Tempranillo prefers mild to hot weather continental climate zones.

To_{uriga Nacional}

High-quality Portuguese grape used as the preeminent variety for making port. Vigorous vines that thrive in searing heat. Small concentrated berries produce dark, fruity and aromatic tannic wines. Grown in Arena Valley Vineyard in southwest Idaho.

Zi_{nfandel}

Identical with southern Italy's Primitivo grape, zinfandel is vinified in many styles including slightly sweet blush wine, red table wine, late harvest dessert wine, sparkling wine and port-style wines. Zinfandel is often characterized as hearty and spicy.

Zw_{eigelt}

Also known as Blauer Zweigelt is the most popular grape in Austria developed by Fritz Zweigelt in 1922. Known for winter hardiness, late bud-break, and early ripening. Fruit driven, light-bodied wine with soft tannins and intense cherry aromas.

Winery	Chardonnay	Gewürztraminer	Muscat	Pinot gris	Riesling	Roussanne	Sauvignon blanc	Sémillon	Viognier
3 Horse Ranch Vineyards	●		●		●				●
Bitner Vineyards	●			●					●
Camas Prairie Winery	●	●	●	●	●				
Carmela Vineyards	●				●			●	
Cinder Winery	●								●
Clearwater Canyon Cellars									
Coeur d'Alene Cellars	●								
Cold Springs Winery	●				●				●
Davis Creek Cellars	●				●				●
Fraser Vineyard									●
Frenchman's Gulch Winery	●								
Fujishin Family Cellars									●
Hegy's South Hills Winery	●				●				
Hells Canyon Winery	●								
Holesinsky Winery	●								
Indian Creek Winery	●				●				
Koenig Distillery & Winery	●				●			●	
Miceli Vineyards & Winery	●								
Parma Ridge Vineyards	●	●							●
Pend d'Oreille Winery	●		●		●				●
Sawtooth Winery	●		●	●	●	●	●		●
Silver Trail Winery	●	●							
Snake River Winery	●				●				
Snyder Winery	●				●				
St. Regulus Unique Wines					●				
Ste. Chapelle Winery	●	●			●		●		
Syringa Winery							●		
Thousand Springs Winery	●								
TimberRock Winery	●				●				
Vale Wine Co.	●				●				
Weston Winery & Vineyards	●				●				
Williamson Orchards & Vineyards					●				●
Woodriver Cellars	●				●		●		

Cabernet franc	Cabernet sauvignon	Grenache	Lemberger	Malbec	Merlot	Mourvedre	Pinot noir	Syrah	Tempranillo	Zinfandel	Wine Country	Pg #
			•				•					52
	•			•			•					36
	•	•		•			•					26
•	•			•	•							66
	•						•					86
			•									28
					•							24
	•			•	•		•					64
	•		•	•			•		•			46
	•						•					89
	•			•								72
				•			•					34
		•			•							91
•	•						•					44
				•			•					68
	•		•	•	•		•					58
	•			•	•		•					38
	•			•								83
	•			•			•			•		82
•	•		•	•		•						22
•	•			•			•					48
	•	•										85
	•	•	•	•			•		•			56
•	•			•			•					70
	•			•		•						81
	•			•			•					42
	•		•	•						•		87
							•					90
	•											80
												88
												84
	•						•					40
												54

REDS

105

Ste. Chapelle Winery

Get the Complete WineTrails Northwest Series!

WineTrails OF WASHINGTON
First Edition
Published December 2007
608-full color pages; 32 WineTrails;
   228 wineries; 1 book
Only $19.95 plus S&H while the
   First Edition lasts!

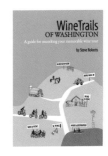

WineTrails OF OREGON
First Edition
Published 2009
Your guide to all things great about
   Oregon wine – travel, taste and experience.
Only $24.95 plus S&H!

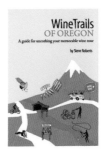

WineTrails OF IDAHO
First Edition
Published 2009
Sip and swirl through the Gem State and
   discover great wines!
Only $16.95 plus S&H!

TO ORDER:
Call **800-533-6165** or order online at
www.winetrailsnw.com/shop

It's easy, it's convenient and the books are signed and personalized
with your message. WineTrail guides are a great gift!

VISIT. TASTE. EXPERIENCE.

Carmela Vineyards

Index

This index covers cities and wineries. Cities are listed in bold. Wineries can be found individually in alphabetical order or under the city in which they belong.

Thousand Springs Winery

Tasting Notes